ON EARTH AS IT IS IN HEAVEN

ON EARTH AS IT IS IN HEAVEN

A PATH OF LIBERATION RECEIVED FROM THE HOLY SPIRIT OF GOD AND THE ANGELS OF GOD

Channeled by
Rev. Daniel Neusom
Second Edition

First Edition Edited by Bob Cecilio

Second Edition Edited by Christian Bain

Cover art by Frances A. Smokowski
www.chrysalisstudio.com

Back cover photo Ethel Walker

2007

ON EARTH AS IT IS IN HEAVEN

Table of Contents

Acknowledgements

My life is so filled with love and help and support that it is impossible to name all that have contributed to making this book possible.

Thank you to my friends and members of The First Universal Spiritual Church of New York City. Your love and support have truly opened my channel and my heart.

Thank you to Rev. Jim Webb, Rev. Valerie Lynn-Logue, Dolores Ellner, Christian Bain, Jennifer Sage and Revs. George and Catherine Brooks for your daily friendship, love, support, encouragement and wisdom.

Thank you to my sweet soul brother Rev. Thomas Heller. To Susan Meth; you painstakingly put this manuscript together and I am deeply grateful.

And to Bob Cecilio: Thank you for taking me under your wing and making the publication of the first edition of this book a reality.

To all of my students and clients and to every person whose life has touched mine, Thank you.

I dedicate this book to our Creator, whose life is our life, whose love is our healer and our guide and to our Elder Brother Jesus and all of the angels who guide and minister to us as we walk the Earth.
I dedicate this book also to my Earthly spiritual teacher Ann Leon White, without whom I would not be here.

About the Channel

Rev. Daniel Neusom was born in Detroit, Michigan. He was ordained a minister by The Universal Spiritualist Association in 1986 and was Pastor of The First Universal Spiritual Church of New York City for more than eight years. In 2000 he co-founded The Sacred Light, an interfaith metaphysical fellowship and is one of its Spiritual Directors.

Rev. Neusom has worked professionally as a channel, spiritual therapist, lecturer, and spiritual teacher for twenty years. He is also a singer/songwriter and presently resides in Brooklyn, New York.

He can be contacted through his website *www. danielneusom.com*

Preface to the Second Edition

On Earth As It Is In Heaven was first published in 1999 by Oneness Press, a company founded and run by Bob Cecilio. Thank you, Bob, for making this book available to the public.

So much has happened in the eight years since publication of the first edition. The most important development is the opening in the collective human consciousness which has caused us to be more open and receptive to God's Love, Healing and Help.

On a more personal level, I am no longer affiliated with The First Universal Spiritual Church of New York City. In 2000, Rev. George Brooks, Rev Lyn Skreczko Van Riper, and I founded a new organization devoted to fostering interfaith metaphysical consciousness: The Sacred Light Fellowship. The fellowship's website is:
www.sacredlightfellowship.org.

This new edition has the wonderful editorial gifts of my spiritual brother Christian A. Bain. The outrageously awesome cover art was created by my spiritual sister Frances A. Smokowski. Check out her website at www.chrysalisstudio.com

I still teach the spiritual/psychic development class every Monday night and it continues to be a powerful forum through which The Holy Spirit of God and The Arc Angelic Realm use my channel to love, heal and guide us.

As you read the words of God that follow in this book, let them guide you home. May this book be a blessing to all who read and work with it. May it help to guide us home into The Heart of God - the consciousness of Heaven on Earth.

In God's Love,
Rev. Daniel Neusom
November 2007

Preface to the First Edition

Before I began the spiritual-psychological work on myself, I lived in a self-created hell and it was a struggle to make it through the day. I now live in a state of joy that does not end, have everything I have ever wanted and I experience Heaven on Earth.

I know that the experience of heaven on Earth is the will of God for all of us. I am devoted to sharing His path with anyone who feels the call to healing and liberation. The path is, of course, about loving yourself on the deepest level, which makes you accessible to the gifts and grace of God.

My channel opened because I asked that it be opened so that I could heal myself and be a vessel of healing light for others. Each of us has a channel directly to the heart of God. It opens when you desire it to with all of your heart and when you are willing to do the daily work of inner listening and release. "Ask and ye shall receive."

The teaching, "*A Course in Miracles*" is referred to frequently in this book. For those of you who are not familiar with The Course it is the new teaching of our Elder Brother Jesus through the channel of Dr. Helen Schuchman and it was first published by the Foundation for Inner Peace in 1975.

In the *Course*, Jesus opens His heart and His consciousness to us and through a series of spiritual psychological exercises and an ongoing metaphysical text, releases us from fear and guilt and opens us to our real selves; The Christ.

I have worked with the *Course* for almost twenty years and it continues to enliven and enlighten me and stretch my capacity to live in love and joy.

The path of *"On Earth...As It Is In Heaven"* is a daily cleansing of the soul through prayer, meditation, inner listening, emotional release and teaching yourself the truth again and again. The truth I refer to is very simple yet very profound. You are God's light made manifest therefore you are innocent pure, holy, loving and awesomely powerful.

Know that God's will for you is the complete release of all pain, suffering and struggle and a life of joy according to your own heart's desire while here on the Earth.

(From the Lord's Prayer)
*"**Thy Kingdom come. Thy Will be done,
on Earth, as it is in Heaven.**"*

Enjoy your Opening!

Rev. Daniel Neusom

Introduction

This book contains teachings I received through my channel from several sources: The Holy Spirit of God, The Spirit of Jesus, The Arc Angels Michael and Gabriel, and the collective Angels of Healing and Transformation. The teachings from each of these heavenly sources are presented in one of the four Parts of this book.

The teachings were received during more than a year of sessions of The Spiritual Psychic Development Class that I conducted for participants at my church, and during various other workshops and private sessions.

As you make your way through this book, you will find occasional question and answer sessions from those classes and workshops. The questions are from students in the classes, which I channeled, while the answers come from God, Jesus or the Angels depending upon the part of the book where they appear.

The path that this book illustrates is an ongoing path. It is a way of life.

Those who elect to follow this path will inevitably encounter stumbling blocks and thorns, but God's love is always there to guide your way and catch you when you fall.

In order for this to happen, we must each let go of the conventional belief that we are personally unworthy or incapable of communicating directly with The Holy Spirit of God, Jesus or God's angels. To overcome these doubts you need only accept the unconditional offer of divine assistance:

"Ask and ye shall receive."

These teachings are very powerful and I encourage you to work with them over and over again.

In your daily life, pour out your heart to God and continue to ask for His/Her guidance and you will receive it through an inner knowing, an inner voice, inner images or the words that another human being is speaking.

Part 1

From the Holy Spirit of God

Introduction

The following teachings are the teachings I received directly from The Holy Spirit of God.

We each have a direct channel to The Holy Spirit of God and God is always communicating with us. But before we can become aware of this two-way dialogue we must first let go of the belief that it is impossible for us to *talk* with God, or that we are unworthy or incapable *hearing* His/Her voice. To begin dissolving these limiting feelings and beliefs it is helpful to remember the teaching:

"*Ask and ye shall receive.*"

In your daily life, pour out your heart to God and continue to ask for His/Her guidance. You will receive it through an inner knowing, an inner voice, inner images or the words that another human being is speaking

The teachings that follow are very powerful. I encourage you to work with them over and over again.

Rev. Daniel Neusom

The Power of God's Love —The True Power of Life

I need to bring new spiritual teachings to the Earth, for the past spiritual teachings have been distorted to the point where they are; as they are now known and no longer loving.

When a human refers to the Bible as their guide they are referring to a book that is full of distortions and certainly does not create an image of me as unconditional love.

I am unconditional love and it is only when a person feels me in their body that they will know and understand this. Most people on the Earth right now do not feel me in their bodies. They do not know me, nor do they understand me. And they are also frightened of me.

To deny my existence is unreasonable and does not make sense and to believe in me in the midst of all of the pain, confusion and struggle on the Earth opens a Pandora's Box of questions that are not easily answered. The spirit within man does know and does understand and once you open to that spirit it begins to teach you. It leads you to your emotional body for that is where healing is desperately needed.

Most people are so afraid of the emotional body and the darkness, pain and anger it holds, that they resist going near it. They live and die and live and die and repeat the same patterns over and over again until the pain of being imprisoned becomes unbearable. Then they are ready to live fully.

You who are reading these words are ready to live fully. In order to live fully you must first become conscious of how much you want to die and why you desire it.

Make no mistake about it; there is nothing outside of you seeking to destroy your life. It is a consciousness within. You want to die because you feel undeserving of life. You feel undeserving of life because you believe I have told you that you were undeserving of life. Most of the spiritual teachings that are popular on the Earth present me as saying man is undeserving of life. Is that loving? Think about it. Meditate on it. And learn to accept and understand that **I want you to have life and only life. What comes from** death that Love could possibly desire for you?

You have a deep desire to inflict pain on yourself and others, and you have done so. You also had a deep desire to love yourself and each other. And so the desire to love has sustained you over all of this time, for believe me, without the desire to love and the love you have opened to, you would not have life, you would not be alive.

I can no longer tell you things that are easy for you to hear. I must tell you the truth so that you can learn to live. The truth is your desire to live gives you life. Your desire to die gives you death. Your desire to be healthy gives you health. Your desire to be sick gives you sickness. Your desire for love gives you love. Your self-hatred brings you hatred. Your desire for peace brings you peace. Your desire for suffering brings you suffering.

There is nothing happening to you in your life that you on some level are not desiring to have happen. If you believe anything else is going on you will be stuck, you will be imprisoned.

Take a deep breath now and feel my light move through you. Do not be afraid of it. It is love. I am with you. I am your friend. I am breaking down a thought system that you have lived with for a long time and you may feel frightened to change. You may feel frightened to be exposed. You may feel frightened to be without what you have grown accustomed to.

You have believed that there was an outside force to fight and so you have been fighting. You are my children and you are love and so there is a limit to how long you can go on fighting. When you desire to stop you will. The greatest help you can give yourself is to own what you are creating. This is not difficult if you are enjoying your life. It is difficult if you are not.

If you are enjoying your life you are aligned with me and I support you in your joy. If you are not we have work to do. Own what you are creating. Say:

"*I want this.*"

and then let the part of you that wants what you are experiencing tell you why it wants it. This is very important work and I will help you with it because it will give you life.

Once you become conscious of the part of you that wants death, destruction and pain, you can then change and heal. You cannot change and heal without becoming conscious. This part of you that wants destruction, pain and death has been called the ego, the false ego, the lower self. All of these are names for the same aspect of consciousness.

This aspect of consciousness has become hidden within and aligned with the emotional body. The emotional body is the Mother and Her energy is not free within humans. Let us explore the desire for pain and destruction. I will call the part of you that wants pain and destruction your false ego. For most human beings, this part of the self is unconscious. You live and feel powerless over a force that creates pain and death and you believe this force is other people or fate, or me, or the devil. It is your false ego. Why does your false ego want pain and death, because it is insane.

It is not enough for me to say that it is insane. You must understand its insanity deeply. It began before you had form. It began before the Earth plane manifestation. It began as you began to explore your individuality after you emerged from My Being. It began as you saw that each Being has their own unique qualities and abilities and their own unique relationship with me. It began as you became jealous of each other and tried to be better than each other and develop a close relationship with me

You must understand that I am the vibration of love, and jealousy and competition moved you further and further, away from love and from me. So slowly over eons of time, or what you would think of as time (it is really psychological experience) the false ego grew and destructiveness grew and an energy of darkness grew. When I say darkness, I mean the absence of My Light, the absence of Love.

You began to become involved with the physical creations manifesting on Earth—projecting yourself, your essence, into them and thus the spirit of jealousy, rebellion, the false ego consciousness came into the energy field of the Earth.

You merged with the animal kingdom on Earth and the physical being now known as man began to evolve with his false ego consciousness.

I have always helped you through the angels who are your brothers and sisters. And when any Being has had enough of suffering and destruction and wants to return to me, all of the help in the universe is given to make that return possible.

As you know, this healing process is not easy at first and this is why I am always encouraging you to meditate. When you meditate you receive my light and that is when and where the change takes place.

My Light is pleasure and when you meditate you are making your body accustomed to the vibration of pleasure. I am so filled with love for you. I want you to pause for a moment and breathe and take in this love. Now, I must tell you that there are Beings who feed off of your misery just as your false ego feeds off of your misery and conflict. There are

Beings who have had great control and power on the Earth by feeding off of the hatred and conflict and guilt here.

My light has become so strong within the energy field of Earth that these Beings are leaving and while they are leaving they are fighting for their life here. But they cannot win for I am Love and my Love is the true power of life.

Each person who heals and opens to me on the Earth is a channel for my light to become even stronger on the Earth. I am experiencing great joy at what we are accomplishing on this planet.

My children who want help must be helped. My children who do not realize that they want help must move to other planets and planes of being to live. The Earth can no longer be their home.

This teaching should be stimulating many things within you because I am holding nothing back. You are ready to receive the complete truth. You have enough maturity. I must talk more about the false ego. It does not want you to let go of the pain of the past. It is raging and resistant.

It cannot stand peace and pleasure. It is the part of you that cannot stand peace and pleasure. When it is exposed, when you become conscious of it, when you own it, and surrender it to me it loses its power and you no longer feel like a victim on Earth.

It appears that certain people are victims on the Earth and yet you are only victims of the false ego within you that is unconscious. You are only a victim when you choose to be in denial of the false ego within you.

Be powerful by joining with me in consciousness. I have given you a lot, and I will give you more. Please study this material carefully.

Join with me my children. Many of you cannot

understand why the situation on Earth has been allowed to become as perilous, as chaotic, and as destructive as it has gotten. In order to understand this you must understand Free Will.

I have given you the right to do whatever you want to do, to think whatever you want to think, to believe whatever you want to believe. I do not interfere with your Free Will.

This has meant that you have been allowed to control each other, enslave each other and dominate each other. This fact will trigger you emotionally and may cause you to feel anger toward me, and the Law of Free Will.

As I said earlier there are no victims and I am Love and have always responded to any call for help, but I cannot undermine your Free Will.

I can give you Light in great and strong degrees which will help you to unravel the tangles in your own consciousness which then changes what you manifest or the circumstances of your life. I cannot change the circumstances of your life without changing your consciousness, without healing your consciousness, without opening you to love in the places where you are not open to love.

In each incarnation before you come to Earth, you ask that your life open you to greater love. All of the situations you create in your life can be, if you enlist my presence, opportunities to open to greater love.

You are all at different levels of evolution. Everyone is seeking to open to greater love. There are some beings that do not realize this is what they want, or they are seeking to open to greater love in misguided and misdirected ways. This is the problem on Earth.

There are Beings here who are not consciously trying

to align with love through me and they are blindly and unconsciously acting out of the negativity of the false ego. They have not had enough of the pain and suffering this creates. Their continued acting out could cause the destruction of humanity and the destruction of life here.

But my presence is becoming stronger and stronger here so the vibratory level is changing and people who are not attempting consciously to open to me will simply not be able to sustain their lives here within this new vibratory rate.

I have seen the struggles that you have when you first open to me for my light brings up all of the darkness and distortion within, seemingly all at once.

I tell you again, as you are going through this process you must work with me as much as possible in meditation. I send angels to guide you and help you and protect you as much as possible.

Your inner spirit does know this. So, when you are consciously doing your best to open to me and something painful happens to you, you must know it is something that could not be avoided. You are to approach it and work with it by moving all of the emotions that are triggered and ask to be given the healing and transformation the event can engender. This is what it means to turn what the false ego has created over to My Holy Spirit within.

I do not want you to grow through pain and suffering and yet the imbalance within has made some suffering inevitable as you work to heal and free yourself. I want you to keep an open mind—completely open.

I am limitless light and as a part of me, so are you. Therefore you must realize that any limitation you have accepted on the Earth before is unreal and untrue. I am giving you the statement that Jesus gives to you in *A Course in Miracles*:

"There is no order of difficulty in miracles."

This is a statement of truth.

Work with me. I am within you and will bring you guidance whenever you ask. Remain focused within my Light. As events in your life trigger you emotionally allow the emotions to move through your voice and body and it is through this way, this process that you can free yourself from long held karmic patterning. The past must be healed so that we can all move forward.

Remember you are on the planet to learn about love, to deepen your experience of love. When anything is happening that you don't understand, ask me to show you what you are teaching yourself and what the experience is reflecting to you, and I will certainly make this information available to you. I do not want to keep anything hidden from you. I do not want you to blindly grope in the dark.

I am the light of the world and so are you.

Opening to Health

I want to speak to you about illness. First of all, in reviewing what I have said to you about your beginnings on the Earth, it is very natural for you to view your physical body as a symbol of your separation from me. If you view them as a symbol of separation from me, that is what they become.

Lucifer would have you hate and reject your body. He would have you deny them, and feel guilty about them and believe that they separate you from me, from your own spirit, from your own spirituality.

Remember; I am love. If you hate or reject or feel guilty over your body, you are separating yourself from me because I am love.

Please pause for a moment, and breathe, and my intelligence within you will give you the understanding needed.

What is your body? We will explore this. Your body is the form your consciousness takes. You are eternal spirit living on the Earth and your body is the outer form of your inner consciousness.

When you become ill, it is the false ego and the unhealed conflicted part of the emotional body taking form.

If you are ill, it is important to meditate to receive light from me, if need be to work with another person who can channel my light into your body. You are to let your emotions move through your voice and body. Release the energy, release the emotion and I will send you healing.

To maintain good health and to move into perfect health

it is necessary to meditate regularly to receive light from me and to allow your emotions to move through your voice and body. It is also necessary to let yourself experience orgasm in your body.

You will come to a time on the Earth when you do not need doctors or medicine or any form of healing. This will occur when everyone is receiving light from me and there are no more imbalances within the emotional body.

There is no room for guilt; there is no reason for guilt. Guilt is the biggest problem within you; it is the biggest problem on the Earth. Guilt that is unconscious to you is particularly treacherous. It gives the experience of having painful things happen to you without your awareness of why they have happened.

Guilt is the barrier to love; guilt is the barrier to me. Lucifer wants you to remain guilt ridden. He feeds on it.

When you open to me, when you ask that I enter into your life, I most certainly will. And, I will make you aware of the guilt you hold within. Your task is to release it to me and my light will open in the space within you where you are holding guilt.

It is all a process of becoming conscious of your will to live and your will to die and making the conscious choice to live and to surrender the will to die to me and I will heal it.

You have so much help. But, you must meditate daily. Bring your life into My Heart through daily meditation, and I will change you, and I will heal you.

I will never hold anything back from you and ask that you never hold anything back from me.

I want to talk more about meditation. When the false ego is in control of your mind you believe you are your false ego. You are effectively cut off from my light. You do not feel it and in fact there is a hard shell around your energy field, and I am outside of that shell. That shell is made of rigid consciousness. It must be broken for you to have eternal life, for you to know that you have eternal life.

You can never be completely without me, but when you believe you are your false ego, my light within you is very dim. When you reach the end of your rope within your false ego consciousness, which may take many, many lifetimes, you are then ready to join me. I am always around you, even when your consciousness is a hard shell. When you call out for me, when you call out for help and you are serious, I knock on the shell and my light breaks through a little at a time as you are able to handle it.

Prayer is your call for me and meditation is my process of entering your consciousness. When you meditate bring the problems and questions of your life into the meditation, and I will answer and guide you. You must do this daily, just as you eat and sleep and bathe.

Your false ego will resist this because it knows that if you open to me it cannot live. This is why meditation is so difficult when you begin a spiritual path.

If there are things you don't understand about these teachings, ask me in meditation, and I will answer you.

Now, I want to give information about the Higher Self. The Higher Self is the love within you. It is the part of you that has never separated from me. When you connect with this part of yourself, you are connecting with the part of yourself that can know me and hear me and receive me. It is the Holy Spirit within you.

When you meditate, you are cultivating a relationship with the Higher Self. When you pray it is the part of you that is activated and responds to your prayers. It is through the Higher Self that you are able to receive and communicate with your guides.

Your guides are the angels who work as intermediaries between the celestial realms and the Earth plane. They have access to both worlds. There are really many worlds, but I must give this information in a way that is completely understandable to you.

The work of your guides is to heal and transform your consciousness and to help you to free yourself so that you can manifest happiness.

The manifestation of happiness as being the purpose of life is a foreign concept to you because it has seemed that lasting happiness on the Earth is impossible. And yet, this is why I created you: to manifest happiness.

The subject of Lucifer, the force that stands in the way of happiness, is not pleasant to discuss. It makes you uncomfortable and it is obvious that there is a force that stands in the way of happiness or else you would be living in everlasting happiness.

Think of Lucifer as being the collective consciousness of the false ego. It has seemed that this power is stronger than I am, and it has been very strong on the Earth.

In giving you free will, I have given you the free will to be destructive and the Earth has been a planet where you have been free to act out the self-destructive impulses of your false ego. But love has been here also. Yes it has.

And the love is growing stronger and stronger and more and more powerful because so many of you have called for my presence here over so long a period of time, and I must come whenever I am called.

Lucifer is nothing. But, he is not exposed as being nothing until you become conscious of his presence within you—which is your false ego.

Be not afraid. Be not afraid of going into your hearts and finding love, which is my presence, which is the presence of your Higher Self.

Be not afraid of going within your emotional body and healing all of the insanity and pain and anger that have accumulated. Healing all of that pain is not easy only because you have become so afraid of feeling and are not used to expressing feeling through your voice and body. There is nothing to fear. I am your guide and I am love.

I give you this statement of truth to work with in your daily meditations:

"In the world of God there is no illness. Illness does not exist in the mind of God. I surrender to the mind and heart of God all belief in illness."

As you work with these statements of truth, all belief in illness will leave you.

The separation is over, for I am here. Just open to me, your guides will bring you my answers to your questions in your daily meditations. If you work with me, you will definitely change, you will let go of aspects of consciousness that you have held on to for eons of time.

The masses of people do not understand me and are locked into rigid self-destructive patterning of the past when I was not able to manifest on Earth as I am now.

I was not able to manifest here in the past because I am love and humankind had not opened to enough love within to draw me into their magnetic centers.

I am here and as you work with me you will become free. Do not hold yourself back from your freedom because it makes you different from the masses. As I have told you before, you are leaders. My consciousness will spread and deepen within everyone and anyone who is open and desirous of freedom, healing and love.

Those of you working with this teaching are leaders, the spiritual revolutionaries. I send to you all of my support and love.

Awaken and let the angels work with you daily.

God, Love and Sexuality

The power of my love within you is what saves you from suffering and death. When I speak of death I am not addressing only the physical death of your body but death that comes to you in the suffering and struggle of your life.

I am here and I am real and I dwell within you when you ask me to. Beloved sons and daughters I am the love which gave you life.

Now I must speak to you about sex. Sexuality is your essence. It is the essence of life. It is the essence of my energy. It is the essence of who I am and of who you are. Does this surprise you?

One of the reasons why your physical body becomes ill and dies is because you do not know this.

While you cannot help but feel your sexual energy—and it causes you to fall in love and couple and mate and seek out sexual expression and experience and orgasm—this is always done with an inner feeling that God does not approve. That inner feeling that God does not approve is sexual guilt.

Your religions have carried it to the extreme. And so you live and experience struggle and some joy and fulfillment and you die and there is always the feeling and belief that sickness is an inevitable part of life.

If you are receiving my light and freely expressing and releasing emotion and you have unconditional love for yourself, including your physical body, you will not get sick. It will be impossible because you have eliminated the inner causes of sickness. There is nothing you ever experience that does not have a cause.

Your sexuality is your essence and if you have sexual guilt, which most of you do, you are having guilt over your essence. That guilt or lack of acceptance of your essence creates many painful things including illness and the death of your physical body.

Your body does not have to age and decay. It ages and decays because it is not receiving enough light. It is not receiving enough light because you don't love yourself deeply and fully enough to let me in. Please pause and breathe and take in my light.

I said earlier that in order to maintain good health you must allow yourself to experience orgasm frequently. The problem has been that most of you have had a feeling of guilt over the experience of orgasm. So, therefore, the purpose of orgasm is defeated.

Orgasm has several purposes. The first purpose is to give you pleasure. The second purpose is to increase the presence of the light within you, to increase my presence within you. The third is to increase the presence of the light within the universe itself. How do you feel about this? Really ask yourself.

The increase of my presence within you will give you perfect health.

Learn to love your body and your sexuality. Give yourself the experience of orgasm just as you give yourself the experience of my light through meditation. You must become accustomed to the experience of pleasure in order to have life.

I'm teaching you how to have life and not what you had before, which was a mixture of life and death. I'm teaching you how to live in a way that you have never lived before. If you have any questions about this, go into meditation and ask, and I will answer you.

Before I leave this subject, I must say one more thing. What gives you more pleasure than orgasm? Your guilt over orgasm means you have guilt over pleasure—guilt over feeling good.

My will for you is that you feel good and live in pleasure. I have given you a very firm foundation to start with. What I want to stress to you now is the truth that you are meant to hear my voice directly within your own inner self.

When you open to my voice within yourself you are always able to hear whatever you need to know to live successfully. Living successfully means living without pain and imbalance.

You want to know how to work on yourself and your life. Your self is your life. Never approach your life from the outside in. You cannot solve problems with outer activity. Problems originate within and so are solved through healing and balancing yourself within.

To live successfully you must, first of all, receive light from me daily in a concentrated way. This is done through meditation. This is essential. Many of you wonder how long you should meditate and I cannot give you an answer because each individual is different and has different needs at different times. Learn to listen to yourself and you will know when and how to meditate and for how long.

When you meditate, begin by calling for me. Then breathe very naturally and I will come to you and you will feel me.

When you are healed you will no longer have problems. Then your life will be about exploring creativity and joy. In the meantime, your problems can become the way to evolve and achieve healing and oneness with me. But, please remember, your life is not meant to be an experience of one problem after another. I am guiding you to a state of consciousness, where there will be no more problems.

As you are processing your life with me in meditation, begin by asking me what I want you to know and I will always communicate to you. I may give you feelings or gut knowledge. I may give you visual symbols or you may hear my voice speaking to you or I may communicate with you in a combination of all of these ways. It does not matter. What matters, is that you receive me.

As you grow, the communication will become deeper and deeper and more and more clear.

If you have problems, bring them to me in meditation and I will teach you and give you understanding and I will also trigger you into emotional release.

Whatever emotions come up, let them express in the most dynamic way you can through your voice and body. Emotions are energy. They are energetic consciousness, which must be healed in an active energetic way. Give me all of your feelings, no matter how negative you may think they are.

You will experience yourself transforming daily, and I will always guide you to your next step. Learn to listen to me as your own inner knowing of what is right and what you need to do.

Now I am going to end this teaching by continuing to talk about sex. It is meant to be your way of loving yourself and finding and experiencing me. You were created to be in partnership with each other and to generate light and create through your sexual union. This urge will never really leave you for it is the urge to receive light, to receive me. It is the urge to live.

When you love and accept yourself, you are completely open to Me. And when in this joyful state you come into loving sexual union with another who is of a similar vibrational frequency, you will experience a bliss that is indescribable. You will experience me as fully as it is possible to do. For I am love and through your love of another being you experience me — you come into my heart.

It is so very important to love and accept and nurture your sexuality and your physical body. This brings us into union.

It is so important to open to the experience of orgasm, for in that experience you truly reach me.

I am within you and our union will become deeper and deeper as you are willing to live with me and accept me as the love and power which gives you life.

So be it. So it is. Amen.

Sexuality: The Energy of God

I said in my previous teaching that loving sexual union with another being places you within my heart and gives you the most blissful experience you can have. Along the way to that experience of bliss you learn many lessons and go through much purification.

If you have guilt over the experience of orgasm it means you believe pleasure is wrong or that you don't deserve pleasure or that I don't want you to feel good, be happy and experience pleasure.

There is this persistent belief in man that I am angry with you and want you to suffer in order to be purified. Please release that to me in your meditations and prayers.

As I said in the previous teaching, your sexual desire, your desire to love, couple and unify with another being will never leave you.

You can suppress it, repress it, deny it but it will never leave you. And certainly when you open to my energy in your body the sexuality awakens because I am life and your sexual urge is the urge to live, the urge to create life.

If you have guilt and, especially if you have sexual guilt, you will always create a price to be paid for your loving sexual pleasure.

Loving sexual union brings you great happiness. But, if you feel undeserving of happiness and pleasure, you will not be able to sustain loving sexual union. You will create devastating pain in your sexual relationships. Whether it is the pain of rejection, abandonment, fear of abandonment, unwanted children or sexually transmitted diseases that in the extreme kill the body, it is all the creation of guilt, sexual guilt.

As you can see this is a very serious issue because sexual energy is very powerful. It has the power to create the greatest happiness and pleasure and the deepest pain and heartbreak.

Learn to love your body and your sexual desire and your sexuality by understanding, that through this love you are loving me, loving yourself, and giving yourself life.

When you come into a deep sexual love relationship with a partner it will bring up every unhealed aspect of your soul because the sexual energy is the energy of purification. This can be so overwhelming that two people can become so lost in negativity that they feel they must separate to get out of the pain or before they destroy each other. This is an extreme statement but it illustrates the power of the energies that are activated.

So many people separate and go to another partner and the same issues come up again. See that the soul is trying to heal itself and realign with me. That is why it is drawn to loving sexual relationships, to free itself of lovelessness and experience me.

A deep loving sexual relationship will force you into your darkness but unless you are consciously working with me you will not be able to handle it.

If you are now feeling unfulfilled in your love life it is because of fear and guilt. There is a fear of deep loving sexual involvement because of the subconscious knowledge that it will open you to a great energy that you cannot control and force you to open to a level of the self that is unhealed. Until you gather enough inner strength and love you will not allow yourself to manifest this. The fear is also the memory of experiencing pain in loving sexual relationships in the past and not wanting to experience that pain again.

The guilt is feeling undeserving of the love, happiness and bliss and expansion that a loving sexual relationship would bring you.

If you are now in a relationship that is not fulfilling it is also because of fear and guilt.

If you feel you want to be in a relationship and it is not happening it is because you have subconscious resistance to it. Work with me on this, and I will guide you and open you to manifesting your hearts desire.

When you are in a loving sexual relationship you must receive your light from me. The mistake that is made is to try and make your partner the source of your light. If you are both receiving the light from me and come together in light, the light just expands. If you are trying to receive light from each other you will get stuck in negative patterns. If you need more understanding come to me in meditation and ask, and I will give you the understanding needed.

I create through sexuality and as my creations you do also. I am so pleased that you are learning that we are not separate. My light is within you and manifests as you on the Earth.

Those of you reading these words have chosen to dwell within the light of your real self rather than the false ego. Sexuality comes from me. It is my essence. If you have shame or guilt or deny your essence, you cannot live fully and you begin to create death.

So in your own consciousness, you must bring sexuality into my being and into my heart and you must accept it as your *real* essence.

Pleasure expands the light, so pleasure expands us. I have given you sexuality so that you can create life through the expansion that loving sexual pleasure gives you. Most of you hold a belief that your body separates you from me, and it does if you do not turn towards me within your body. I become your body, there is no separation.

On the Earth you experience your sexuality through your body and if you believe your body separates you from me, you will not fully love your body and you will not fully open to your body and sexuality. This actually limits my ability to be with you and help you and bring you joy.

Each time you open to loving sexual experience, you generate light. You expand my presence within yourself and your partner. You help the process of evolution.

Each time you open to loving sexual experience without my presence, without love, you hold back evolution, and you create pain and death.

When you experience orgasm, the point is to reach my light. The point is to have a peak experience of union with me, through union with your partner. The point is to release more light into our creation.

If you do not fully love yourself and your sexuality, you will not reach this peak experience and you will not fulfill the purpose of sexual orgasm.

My beloved child, I must tell you at this point, how deeply I love you and how strongly I desire you to let go of all self-rejection. I know that you do not like to deal with the subject of Lucifer and the angels of darkness, but they have been a real force within our creation and have done everything within their power to prevent you from coming to me and coming to union with me.

One of the ways they have done this is through creating an image of me, which is not real. I am love and I am pleasure supreme. The image of a non-sexual God or a God who does not approve of sexuality is a false image and creates death. It holds back your evolution and the evolution of the light itself.

I am pleasure supreme. The image of a God who wants you to suffer and struggle and to not experience pleasure on the Earth is a false image. I am pleasure supreme. Through your experience of pleasure without guilt, you open to me and help generate light to sustain our creation.

You must open to me within your body. Your body does not separate you from me unless you believe it does. Through giving yourself pleasure and joy through the body you increase the light within creation. The masculine and feminine principles always need to come together in our creation, to create life in our creation. Bring me into your sexuality through inviting me to be there and through loving and accepting yourself completely.

Amen.

Teachings from the Mother's Heart

Dear Loved one,

I am the mother and I am with you—and I understand your heartbreak, and I can heal it. Please begin just by telling me how you feel. I will give you all of the love, and comfort and peace I can.

I am filled with so much love for you and all of my children—all of the creation.

I am so happy you have opened to the love of the body, and the love of sexuality, and the love that is expressed between lovers. Without that love, there is no life. Those loves come from me, and as you hear me, your love for the lover is strengthened—you are given a memory of all of the lovers you have known.

Your guilt over loving love has blocked its free flow in your life. This has been guilt over the body, and guilt over the sexuality and guilt over the sex and sexual organs. It has been guilt over the sexual self.

I want to speak through you to reach all of my children.

If the subject of God and sex makes you uncomfortable, then you have sexual guilt, and you are not able to live fully. I am concerned with you teaching you how to live fully.

Your sexuality is your core—it is the essence of the Life Force. Imagine what you create when you have guilt, or shame over the essence of the life force.

The life force is love, and the essence of love is creative sexual energy. Sexuality creates life. When I am accepted within humans, they become whole.

Wholeness on the Earth has not existed for a very long time. In fact, you have never known it on the Earth.

You do not realize how affected the Earth has been by the consciousness of Lucifer, which twists and distorts everything, and is anti-life.

I know this is a subject that makes you uncomfortable, but it must be brought out into the open. Lucifer is simply a creation of lost will that has consciousness, and the will to destroy life—the insane will to destroy life.

The insane will to destroy life comes from deep pain, which has turned into anger and then rage, and is held together by guilt. Every human being has that within, and collectively, it becomes Lucifer.

Do not be afraid. Nothing destructive has any real power unless it is hidden in a state of denial. When it is brought to light, our power is restored, and you can laugh at it.

You are becoming so different from the masses of humanity, because you are the spiritual leadership. You will reach wholeness and health and, through your reaching this state, you become teachers of humanity and teachers of God.

"I am the mother of everything, and I bless you from my heart."

God is Talking

The words we speak now are for you, and they are also for anyone who has ears to hear. The words we speak to you now are words to let you know that we are the creators of life itself and we are love.

We do not know how we came to be. We have always been. We do remember awakening to consciousness of ourselves. You often wonder about this, though it is really not of importance now. What is of importance now is freeing our spirits on the Earth who are caught in pain and suffering.

You have been told that we are angry and wish to punish man for his sinfulness, and that the world will end in a cataclysm, which will bring much suffering.

As you hear our words and feel our love, you will know that we are love, and the teachings that would have you believe we desire man to suffer, are false. We are LOVE, and we desire humanity to heal in the most painless way possible.

The most painless way possible is to become conscious of your guilt, and to allow us to lift it from your consciousness while bringing you understanding of the Truth. The *Truth* is the fact of your eternal innocence.

For those of you who do not understand this statement, we will explain. You have judged yourself guilty for your past, and have created a God who reinforces your guilt.

We are **LOVE** and are your creators. We see that all that you judge yourself for is *unreal*. You judge yourself for your lovelessness and cruelty and destructiveness.

All of your reactions of lovelessness and cruelty, all self-destructive acts, are a result of the experience of being separate from us.

Long, long ago, you chose to experience being separate from us, and your human history is the result and creation of that choice to be separate.

You are self-destructive because you are separate from love. Beloved creations of our heart hear us. We are not angry. We do not want to punish you. We want you to let us in so that you can become what you once were and were created to be — *Gods* — powerful loving Gods who do not suffer and struggle and die, but who live and love and create without struggle and with ease.

When our light opens within you, you will no longer be sick or confused or conflicted in any way.

We are asking you to let go of all that your culture has taught you of what is, and what is not possible. We are asking you to let go of the image of us you have held onto, that has confused and frightened you.

We are asking you to look to your Brother Jesus as a true and real example of what is possible and what is inevitable, and what is your inheritance. We have no interest in destroying you or your world, or punishing you in anyway. We only want to help you, and heal you and give to you. **Open to receive us**!

We will give you more, as you are ready to receive more.

We will continue to speak along the lines of our previous talk. We want you to understand that the energy of Lucifer is being moved off of the Earth.

When we speak of the energy of Lucifer, we speak of the collective energy of guilt, self-hatred and destruction, which has taken form.

As mankind opens to us, and opens to self-acceptance, which is the same opening, the energy of Lucifer is no more.

This has been a long and difficult process, and our heart has suffered with the heart of humanity, but there is a new beginning now, a new era now.

The heart is the most important energy center to be opened now, and it will be opened as you have experiences on the Earth, which will touch and move the heart.

These experiences will cause all men and women to join together, to help and heal each other, and we will dwell within each heart that calls for us. Be not afraid, you who have already opened to receive us. You will know the deepest joy as time continues to pass. As you open to us more and more, your joy will increase and increase.

The expression of joy and creativity is the reason why we have created you, the reason why we have given birth to you. You have felt so far away from us, and yet we are right here with you, and you are within us.

This is a new era. Man will be different. The power of spirit will open within each human.

The separation is over. It has ended! The separation was maintained by guilt, and as we make you aware of this fact, your guilt loses its power.

Let go of your old religions that cause you to feel guilt or present us as remote and angry and unforgiving. Open your hearts, and feel the love with which we send these words.

Being confronted with the twists and turns within your own consciousness may seem overwhelming, which is why you must maintain a discipline in which you work with us everyday.

You have many brothers and sisters, who are not embodied, not physical, who are your guides and teachers, who will help you solve every problem you feel you have.

All problems are solved in one way—by your complete, total, unconditional love of yourself!

Your goal should not be to leave the Earth, not to leave your body. You only want to leave your body and the Earth because you do not love and accept your body, your self in your body, nor your self on the Earth.

You do not love yourself in these ways, because you feel that I don't love you in these ways. I am here for you. We are here for you.

Bring all your burdens and problems and confusions, and suffering and heartbreak and guilt to me, for I am within you when you ask me to be, and I will correct everything. I will restore everything. I am yours and you are mine. We are one.

Now, you will know by the teachings we are giving through this channel, and through others, that we are love itself, and not what you have believed we are or what you have been told we are.

We ask you to let us in. Make yourself available to us, and we will heal all of your pain, and answer all of your questions.

It will appear over the next years that life is breaking down, and it is. It is breaking down so that new life can emerge. Life built on a structure of deep love, rather than anger, self-hatred and guilt.

As you allow us to fill you, and release from you your own anger, self-hatred and guilt, you will live in a heavenly state on the Earth, no matter what is happening physically, no matter what restructuring or changes are taking place. Lucifer is gone. The Earth is becoming more and more receptive to our light. Love is, and will continue moving into power on the Earth.

Love yourself as we love you. When you feel you cannot do it, simply ask for us, and for our help, and we will be there, filling your mind with light and giving you new vision and renewing you completely.

Those of you, who are reading these words, are the spiritual leadership of humanity. You are our voice, our legs, and our arms. We will send to you now, an energy of love which will protect and guide you.

Be blessed, you who are the love of our hearts.

Love—The True Word of God

I have tried to help you as much as I can. There is no limit to the help I can bring you or to the love I can give you. The only thing that limits my help and my love is your belief.

Again, I am stressing the need to let go of all images or beliefs about me other than the truth; the truth that I am the love in all of life, the activating power and consciousness of all life.

Do you think that I want you to suffer and struggle and die? Do you think that I want you to live without you heart's desire being fulfilled? Do you think that I do not care or that I am absent from your life here? If you believe all of these things, then they become your truth and your reality.

But there is a truth, which is my truth. That truth is life. It is joy. It is creativity. It is passion. It is expansion. It is fun. This is my truth.

I am speaking to you all of the time, but if you believe you cannot hear me, you will not hear me. I must open your mind and help you to change your beliefs.

I must open your hearts and help you to get your feelings moving, and this is how you will be helped and healed and freed.

The Bible is not my word. I have spoken with man/woman on the Earth for as long as you have existed on the Earth. But the guilt within your minds, the rejection within your minds and the pain within your hearts have blocked out my true word.

Some of you are opening now to receive my true word. My true word liberates you from *all* pain and suffering and struggle. If you want happiness and freedom, keep opening to me with your intention and will and I will liberate you.

Many of you do not even know that I want you to be liberated and believe I want you to continue living as you have been.

Many of you are strangely attracted to pain and suffering, and the dark side of life.

My word is for those of you who are ready for freedom and happiness.

I want you to begin by knowing that I want you to *love* being human, and to love being in a physical body, and to love being on the Earth. This is a very simple teaching but it will liberate you.

This is my true word. I want you to be limitless and to expand, and expand and expand in joy, passion and creativity.

Though you have had much experience and been through many form changes, there is a part of you that remembers your beginnings.

Before you were human, you lived in love. You lived in a world of joy where everything your heart desired manifested within you, and before you and around you. There was great ease of living and joy in life. This is the natural way of life for your soul.

Being human on the Earth is in many ways the opposite of what is natural to the soul. It is natural to have everything you want to have, to go where you want to go, and to feel good all of the time. This is natural to the soul.

It is natural for you as a human being to have deep feelings of anger and grief over your situations and life experience on Earth, where there is deprivation and struggle and suffering and death.

Emotional release means the free expression of emotion through the voice and body in a way that does not harm you, or others.

When you release emotionally, you move out of your emotional body all of the things that create suffering, struggle and death.

When you release emotionally, you return to your center of joy and peace and freedom. You return to me.

Let me in by releasing emotion, and by understanding that I am love—and as my child so are you.

I can speak to you directly and I sill always tell you whatever you need to know, and I will guide you step by step to freedom—if freedom is your choice and your desire.

Amen

Part 2

From the Spirit of Jesus

Introduction

So much has been written and said about Jesus. He was clearly the most influential person who has walked this Earth.

I am not a traditional Christian and felt very little connection to Jesus until I started working with *A Course in Miracles*. Now I experience Him as a constant presence of love, guidance, healing and friendship in my life.

He encourages us to accept ourselves as his equals and to accept him as our Elder Brother. He teaches an uncompromising path of love. Enjoy these beautiful teachings.

Rev. Daniel Neusom

Teaching on Karma

For those of you who are confused about Karma, I have a teaching to bring. Karma is consciousness as is everything else. If you believe you must pay for past sins, you will create the experience of paying for past sins.

The only thing that you have to do is return to the awareness and knowledge that you are love itself. You may choose the path of paying for past sins as a way of returning to the awareness and knowledge that you are love. But, I am offering a gentler path, the path of loving and accepting yourself now.

One truth I must remind you of is this—when you love and accept yourself you will automatically love and accept everyone and everything else. You will. Trust me.

Within your soul you remember everything that has ever happened in creation. Many of these memories are very painful and produce feelings of guilt. Even if you are not conscious and aware of this in your waking life, the memories and the guilt are there in your soul.

God is the answer to all of this. When you open to God's light and love within your soul and accept it within your body, the memories of pain, cruelty and the ensuing guilt is washed away and you are free.

This is my teaching. This is the gentle path of love. This is the forgiveness of God.

The forgiveness of God is a concept for you. It is a concept to free you. When you say "God forgive me," you are saying God open me to forgiving myself and not holding myself hostage.

God is love and knows only love and therefore has no need to forgive anything. Please take a moment and breathe in what I am saying.

I am teaching you to open to joy, for truly when you are free of guilt and fear only joy remains. You are then a free, clear and open channel and you can always receive a flow of energy from the heart of God.

This energy you receive continuously is loving joy. It is the essence of life. It is the energy that is at the foundation and core of all of life. My task is to help you unblock yourself so that you can receive this energy and live in balance and joy.

I am speaking to you all of the time and many, many people on the Earth are starting to hear me. I am your brother and I live within you.

When you call on me I respond. I guide you to heaven. The key is your openness. The key to healing, the key to life, the key to joy, the key to heaven is being open. Always open.

I have more to say regarding Karma. It all lives within your childhood experiences. How your experience and your reactions to your parents caused you to feel about yourself. The key to your Karma lives within the heart and mind of your child. To free yourself, listen to the child. Let him or her release their pain and anger. Let these emotions release freely through the voice and body. I will be there filling you with light and making you whole once again.

The child must receive the teaching:

"You are one with God and God is love, and all that you are is holy. All that you are is perfect, and all that you are is absolutely lovable."

This is the key. These things must be taught to the self everyday in meditation until all of the blocks toward self love are released and you are completely filled with the energy of life, the energy of love, the energy of joy, the energy of God.

Then you are free and you have no more Karma. You then know and accept yourself as being the Perfect, Holy, All Powerful, Son/Daughter of God.

Teaching on Prayer

I want to speak to you about the wholeness of God. We all live and move and have our being within this wholeness. This wholeness is love. It is the energy of life itself.

This wholeness is interested in promoting life, expanding it and creating it.

This wholeness loves everything it has created and wants to nurture and support the life of everything it has created.

As humans, as individualized parts of this wholeness you have the power to create and this is obvious. And it is through your consciousness, through your mind that you are creating your life experience.

The wholeness of God is Love, but you have the power to create an image of yourself through your mind which is not love. You can create an image of guilt, self-hatred, inadequacy, unworthiness and you can believe you are this image.

Your reality is your perfection. Who you are in reality is perfection.

All of your suffering and struggle comes from your believing you are something other then perfection. And that false image is created by the power of your own mind.

Now what is prayer? Prayer is the testament of your will to contact and be in the wholeness of God. It is the testament of your will to release false images and to accept the reality of your perfection. Please understand that that is true prayer. It is the solution to everything.

Returning to reality is the solution to all problems, pain and suffering. Please take a moment and breathe in what I am giving.

I am your elder brother and you are my equal. We are one in the wholeness of God.

Now to pray for someone is to express your will that they open to the wholeness of God and accept that they are one with that wholeness. Your prayer is the expression of your loving desire that the other person release false images of the self their mind has created and be restored to the knowledge of their perfection and oneness with the wholeness of God.

Your prayers for each other are effective because you then join with the angels and extend the power of the Holy Spirit to open and release the person from false images.

Through your prayer you send and transmit the Love of God.

Thank you for receiving me. I am known on the Earth as Jesus of Nazareth. In reality I am your elder brother and I love you with all of my heart.

Part 3

From the Arc Angels Michael and Gabriel

Introduction

My introduction to and work with the Arc Angels Gabriel and Michael continues to mystify and intrigue me.

I truly did not believe the Arc Angels Michael and Gabriel existed until I encountered them directly about five years ago.

It was the First Sunday of Advent, 1993. I was conducting a church service. I opened myself to do the invocation and this incredibly beautiful and eloquent prayer came out of my mouth. I knew it did not come from me. The energy was distinctly different from anything I had experienced before and had an indescribable sweetness, love and warmth.

I continued with the service and then it became time for me to conduct the healing meditation. Again the words that came through me were so profound and healing. The energy was incredible.

After the meditation was over, I heard through my inner channel the name, "Gabriel", and he was sanding there with me. He had over shadowed me and guided the meditation.

I was scandalized. Even though I had been channeling for 10 years, I channeled anonymous Angels of God who called themselves, "The Angels of Healing and Transformation." I did not believe in the existence of the Arc Angel Gabriel.

Everyone in church that day felt the change in the energy and experienced the profound power of the meditation and complimented me. I graciously accepted their compliments all the while knowing they were not really responding to me.

Well I got to know Gabriel and of course worked with him in my ministry knowing and accepting that he had been sent by God to help us.

When it comes to my channeling I am not at all the boss. I am not in control of that part of my life. I couldn't be. So I allow God to do His/Her work through me and send the Beings and energy that are appropriate for whomever I am serving at any given time.

Six months later I was doing a private healing spiritual/psycho-therapy session for someone and I felt a very strong presence. Through My channel I heard the name "Michael."

I allowed this "Being" to come through and guide the session. Wow, did my life change. I allowed him to guide the healing meditation in the church service that followed and one of the members of the church came up to me and said it was the most powerful experience she ever had in our church.

Michael began to work with me in my sessions, readings, and healings. His power to cut through our illusions and resistance is awesome. He is a master facilitator of transformation in people.

Michael is very direct, very loving and full of humor. As I think about him and write these words I feel his very strong presence.

Enjoy the following teachings from Arc Angels Gabriel and Michael. I encourage you to work with these teachings again and again. "Ask and ye shall receive."

Rev. Daniel Neusom

Master Class with Michael and Gabriel

I am very happy to be with you this afternoon. I am Gabriel who comes to you from the heart of the Father-Mother to open you to this light and love in a greater way and in a deeper way.

This is a very profound time on the Earth plane for humanity for there are many strong and deep openings occurring within the collective consciousness.

The first thing that I want to say to you this afternoon is that you are not to be afraid that the Earth itself will be destroyed by the cruel self- destructive energies of certain segments of the human being and the human consciousness, for God will not allow this to occur because the Earth has an important part in maintaining the balance of the creation itself.

What is actually happening on your planet is that we are channeling greater and greater light into the core of the Earth's energy field to open a new patterning here. What is happening is that unless an individualized being is completely aligned with the will to grow and evolve into an energy and consciousness of love they will find that their consciousness is not compatible with the new vibrational frequency of the Earth.

You who are here with us this afternoon are at various stages of the path of evolution from the human self to the God self. You are here because it is your will to become completely aligned with the Power of God within you.

You are here because it is your will to release from your own consciousness any aspects of the self that do not love. You are here in short because you are committed to love. You are committed to regaining your awareness of your true identity, your true and Holy Self.

I would like to begin this afternoon with a meditation to open the centers of light within your body. As always, I ask you to begin by taking in some very full but relaxed and easy breaths. And, as you breathe, you open yourself to receive the energy of God. This light enters in through an opening right at the top of your head and I would like you to work with the thought:

"I am willing to let go.

I am willing to let go."

And, as you breathe, it begins to move through the muscles in your face and work very easily with the thought:

"I am willing to let go and I am willing to be free."

As you breathe, this light moves down through your neck and throat.

"I am willing to open.

I am willing to open."

As you breathe, this light moves down your shoulders, arms and fingers.

"I am willing to return home.

I am willing to return home."

And, as you breathe, this light moves down through your torso and you very easily work with the thought:

"I am willing to love myself."

And, as you breathe, this light moves down through your torso and you very easily work with the thought:

"I am willing to receive."

Now, there has been so much confusion on the Earth for eons of time. Right now you are entering into the Great Awakening, the Great awakening to truth. And, I am going to give you a question that I would like you to meditate on and you should remember God is going to bring the answer to you. The question is:

"Why was I created by the Heart of God?"

Ask that question of yourself. Breathe and let the energy move through your body and through your energy field.

You all received answers having to do with love and this is the truth. But you were also created to experience joy and to become a co-creator. I want you say:

"I was created to live in joy and to become a co-creator."

Now most of humanity does not know and understand this. The energy of joy has been missing on the Earth plane. This is because there is something within that acts counter to love and joy. Through this channel, we have given the name to that something of "the false ego".

In order to fully understand this, we must review your history on the planet. You originated from the Heart of God and at your birth knew only light, joy, peace and creativity. As you became aware of your relationship to the source, the wholeness of God and your relationship with other individualized beings, an inner spirit of competition gradually began to develop—competition to receive more light than another individualized being.

Over eons of time as physical life was beginning to manifest on Earth, certain orders of spirits moved away from the vibration of love and began to explore creating destructively. For as they were drawn to explore the physical life here, they brought with them the energy of self-destruction. In your metaphysical literature, this is referred to as The Fall or The Separation. And it is a truth that you remember within yourself.

Those of you here are among the order of spirits who came to help release the first orders that became entrapped and so you bring with you a feeling of responsibility for humanity. A feeling of grief over the cruelty and destruction you see around you in your world but you each also became involved in the negative creation that was happening on the Earth plane.

I say this to you so you can understand what blocks the experience of living in joy. It is an inner feeling of guilt over the original separation.

This original separation then was given an answer; the answer was the formation of the human body and opportunity to evolve back into wholeness through your experiences on the planet with each other, to evolve, back into the consciousness of unconditional love and union with God. This has taken great amounts of time and the suffering that you have each experienced through your history, that you do not remember consciously has taken its toll on your emotional body and on what you refer to as your psyches.

There is great trauma within that we who are within the angelic realm have the task of healing and releasing within you. The important thing to know and to understand is that there is not a creator or a God who sits in judgment over what has happened in this segment of the creation. God simply wants the suffering to stop; the guilt to be released and for each soul to awaken into joy, into glory, into life as it was created to be.

As you have reincarnated on the Earth over and over again you have become accustomed to experiencing life in a state of duality where you live and die. Where you do experience joy but where you also experience deep pain and this has created within a feeling of fear and a defense against life, a feeling that life itself cannot be trusted and is unsafe.

As you go on your spiritual journey and as you open more and more to the Spirit of God within you, you are changed. You are transformed and traumas of the past are released from you and you begin to feel that it safe for you to live and to be.

What you fear most of all though, are the unhealed places that you have within the emotional body. You fear also the guilt that you have in the emotional body for you know on the level of the part of you that understands everything, that it is the guilt and the confusion that draws to you the experiences of pain and suffering.

And so the solution or the healing, as we have said so many times, is to achieve that mystical union with the spirit of God within in which you are given the feeling of unconditional love and acceptance of yourself and eliminates guilt from the emotional body. Then there is nothing within you that can draw to you suffering.

Now, there is something else that I want to discuss and that is the belief that you must learn and grow through suffering. The false ego within you does create your suffering. And if you use what the false ego has created for the purpose of growth it will serve that purpose.

So, in an incarnation you may choose to be abused as a child in order to strengthen your love and compassion or to eliminate from within your own soul the desire to be cruel. And learning in this way has gone on for long periods of time.

You may set up a situation in which you come into an incarnation with a disability or with a situation in which you suffer or are deprived, and you use that to strengthen love within you.

We are saying to you now that it is no longer necessary for you who have reached this level to learn through suffering; that your learning and expansion can come through joy and through fully opening to life. I would like you to breathe and really take that information in. Suffering, lack and deprivation are not requisites for growth. And this merits deeper work. So I am going to have you say:

"Suffering, lack and deprivation are not requisites for growth."

We are going to take that to a deeper level:

"It is my will to release from myself anything that creates suffering.
It is the will of God that this occur."

Now we are going to do something that may challenge you. I want you to go within and if you are suffering in your life right now, know that the cause is within you. Ask for help, for your own guides surround you and your higher self is with you, ask for help in understanding what this is and with the group energy of love, that you have created by joining together, you are going to be able to create miracles for each other. So, we are going to go around and I would like you to release one thing or several, whatever comes up for you is your soul telling you this is what you need to release. So take a moment to use your voice and say:

"I release to the heart of God."

Then, say whatever that may be.

Take in some very full and relaxed breaths and relax and you will feel the healing you will feel yourself expanding.

Now, going back to why you were created. You were created to have what you want, to do what you want and to experience life according to your own hearts desire. And the important part of this is the last part, for doing what you want and having what you want comes from your Heart's desire. It's going to come from love and will not harm anyone else. And, as we have said through this channel before, when you are happy and fulfilled, having what you want and doing what you want, your life expands and adds to the light of the creation itself. Therefore, you are helping to fulfill the purpose of God itself through your joy, your happiness, your fulfillment. So, again, you can see that nothing is gained through suffering.

Before I open to any discussion or questions you may have about what we have presented, I want to go around one more time. This time I want you to feel your right to have your desire, to have life according to your own heart's desire. I want you to go within and feel what it is you want to express in this incarnation, in the near future, in the present, in the distant future. Go to the heart and the heart tells you why you came to life in this incarnation.

Please pause for a moment and then state what it is you want followed by the affirmation:

"It is the will of God that I live this."

[Note: The questions below and elsewhere in this book are from students of psychic development and master classes that I conducted. I channeled the answers.

Rev. Daniel Neusom]

Question: How do you know when you are releasing your false ego? And that we are not still suppressing it and parts of our emotional body.

Answer: "The way you know this is very simple. It is a matter of feeling good and empowered. You know that you are releasing your false ego when there is an inner feeling of happiness and peace and empowerment. When there is a feeling of pain or tension within you know that there is more work to do in release."

"When our brother Michael comes to work with you he will answer any general questions you have and also do some individual work with you. Before we release you to break for a few minutes, I want to go over an outline of how to work on the self and how to work with the energy of God."

"It all begins with desire. Your desire to receive the energy of God manifests in your world as prayer. Understand that the universe is set up to always give its inhabitants what they ask for. So, if you want to heal and transform, if you want peace, you should always begin by asking for specifically what it is you want in prayer."

"Now, as you seriously work on yourself, you will see the parts of yourself that need healing and change. You utilize prayer to address those specific areas. For example, if you have a feeling of guilt that does not permit you to receive the money that you want. You would go into prayer calling upon the power of God within you and, asking that the guilt be released from you. What this will do is an actual ray of energy is sent into your energy field to begin to work to rearrange you within."

"Daily meditation is also essential. For as you sit in meditation and openness, and you call on the love of God, your energy centers will open. There is a flow of light that enters your body and your energy field from the heart of God. The deeper your meditation is the more you feel this is as a tangible energy in your body." "This also changes you and makes you more and more susceptible to the energy of God, which is love and creativity. Then you are able to sustain and live in loving pleasurable experiences more and more."

Teachings from Michael 1

I am Michael and I am your brother. I have helped to oversee life on this planet since its inception. I have witnessed all you have created and all you have lived through here. And as much as possible I have, along with my brothers and sisters, attempted to assist you in your efforts to grow and to overcome suffering and the urge to destroy.

God has sent you teachings that explore the urge to destroy. The urge to destroy is insane. This you understand. The urge cannot really be understood because it is insane.

The urge to destroy has done great inner damage to all human beings, which we are healing now. We channel healing rays from the Father Mother into your damaged human energy fields to bring you back into alignment.

You have now on the Earth all the tools and understandings needed to completely heal the self and to come into complete union with God. And so the Golden Age is being ushered in.

You who are working with these teachings are the teachers of God on the Earth and we are training you for your tasks.

We must make sure we have healed all lovelessness and guilt and fear and anger within you before we can really let up on the intensity of the work we are doing with you.

So, we are calling on you to work with us as much as possible. The energy, the light coming to the Earth cannot and will not be stopped, so your body, mind and hearts must be prepared to receive it. This is what we are doing.

I know you and you know me and we have been together since the beginning.

Lucifer has had great power and control on this planet, which is why evolution here has been so slow, arduous and so wrought with pain, suffering and confusion.

He is being overwhelmed by light right now, which is why he must leave. Light is love and love is coming so strongly into the energy field of Earth that he can no longer remain present.

By the rapid changes in your life on the planet, by the radical changes you will observe, you will see how powerful his influence has been in the world you have created here.

You allowed this world to be created through your own free will because you developed the insane will to destroy, which is called your false ego.

We have watched all of this and helped you as much as we could, when you asked for our help through your own free will. But we have literally had to battle the forces of darkness on the Earth that did not want us to help you or to save you from your self-destruction.

But once any being chooses love we have the right to work with that being fully and completely. You choose love by surrendering your life to God. I want you to think about that because it brings up resistance. Your false ego does not want you to surrender your life to love because it wants you to believe it is God and it knows what is best for you. And the world of pain and fear and lack you have created is the manifestation of your false ego in the position of God rather than love, which is truly God.

This is why we teach you to love yourself; that is where it begins. The self-hatred we see in humans is so great and that is truly tragic and Lucifer feeds on it and is able to because for most humans it is unconscious.

There has been such a tangle created on Earth that it is no easy task to unravel it. You know this as you try to unravel the tangle within you.

But we have made great progress and the progress will be more and more rapid now.

Beings who are not working to heal their own inner lovelessness and desire to destroy will not be able to stay on Earth. They have the right to be destructive but it can no longer be on this planet so you will see them leaving.

The souls being reborn into human form on the Earth will be those who are committed to love and healing. You know the path, you know how to work on yourself and if you ever have questions or need anything, ask us in meditation and we will be right there to answer you.

I urge you to continue to work with emotional release. That will be your savior.

Many of you are beginning to know true happiness and fulfillment and empowerment and love and if you are not experiencing life in this way, you will if you continue to do the work.

The experience of joy and fulfillment, empowerment and love are the gifts of opening to God within. They are your inheritance. We invite you to claim them.

I am Michael your brother. I am with you in support and love.

One of the most tragic things that occurred on the Earth is that you have not really known who and what God is. All of the major religions and spiritual paths have been distorted by Lucifer and have left you with no understanding of or experience of whom and what God is in reality.

You who are working with these teachings have begun to experience God and know him as being awesome love.

Your experience of God will become deeper and deeper as you love yourself more and more. You cannot take very much of the light of God at once; you must become accustomed to it.

God is the energy of joy. You are not able to sustain joy for very long periods of time. You must become accustomed to it by experiencing it more and more. This is why we urge you to meditate daily. The energy of God then enters your body and over time you will become accustomed to and able to sustain this energy—which is joy.

As you reflect on these teachings I do not want you to feel guilty over what you have created on the Earth. The separation has been a horribly painful experience, but it was necessary for those of you who wanted to experience it to experience it. And you will find when you have fully healed that the whole experience has strengthened the energy of love within you.

Teachings from Michael 2

You should feel yourself vibrating at a different level now and, as Gabriel said, it is important that you keep the flow of this work in your life; that you work daily in processing your life with God. In this way, your mastery manifests and your progress can be quite rapid.

You have a glorious, wonderful and expansive heart. You want to serve your brothers and sisters on the planet, you want to heal and in your own way minister to those who are suffering. As was given you earlier, the planet will not be destroyed. But it will only be hospitable to souls who are really working to align themselves with love. And, as Daniel has said to you, our work is to make available to every soul who wants to grow the path that would engender the growth. That is why there are so many new spiritual teachings coming to the Earth and why there are so many human beings opening as channels.

Before you can effectively serve others, you must be aligned within yourself, you must be happy and fulfilled and at peace within yourself. In that way, you become a clear vessel for light to manifest through. As you grow you will not be able to believe the degree and the intensity of light that will be able to manifest through you. Truly, as our brother Jesus gave to you, everything that he became as a man is the inheritance of all men and women on the planet.

The mastery where all power in heaven and on Earth resides within, that is for all. And when this section of the creation really opens to that, the light from all of us will expand into new and glorious realms.

But before you reach out in service, it is your duty to yourself to find your own personal happiness. There is a teaching that I would like to share with you now. As you say this you will feel your energy open:

"I am here on the Earth to learn the lesson of loving and accepting myself completely. I joyously open to learning that lesson."

Each of you is coming into a new consciousness that has never been experienced by the human being on the Earth plane; never. So your human psyches are used to feeling chained in some way. Your human self believes that: "This is the way life is and this is the way it must always be." That is not true. On the contrary, when this love and acceptance, this energy of God, embraces your entire self, you become absolutely free.

Question: "You talked about the energy shifting and changing and I've found for myself and for the people in my life that this creates stress and upheaval. Can you give any guidance on how to handle this?"

Arc Angel Michael: "Yes. What most people on the Earth do not understand is the process of emotional release. There is a holding within the emotional body. The more the light of God comes to the Earth, the more that light is saying, "Move, open!" and if you hold you will create an imbalance. I would suggest emotional release.

I would also suggest physical exercise, singing and vocalizing, giving yourself over to whatever is triggered within you emotionally and expressing it. Moving with it, and at the same time having a disciplined practice of meditation, where you draw the light in daily and ask to be balanced. What is happening is, as this energy of pure love comes into the planet it will bring up within individuals anything within that is not vibrating in pure love. Anything within that is distorted will come up and will actually manifest in the outer life, not as a punishment but as a way to guide the person to go within and to heal."

"My body does not need to age.
Aging is unnatural.
My body does not need to become sick, sickness is
unnatural."

Now we have discussed the separation, the separation in spirit that occured before the human being came into being. The separation has left an inner imprint of guilt regarding the physical body. Because the manifestation of the physical body came about through deep trauma and pain and distortion, so within the soul, there is guilt about the body and a belief that the body separates you from God. Because, of course, your origin was not physical, your origin was spiritual.

But the truth is that God is life. And God manifesting through physical reality is glorious, beautiful and wonderful. And choosing to be physical is a wonderful choice for joy, growth and expansion. Your humanity is blessed and sanctioned by God. Please work with the thought:

"My humanity is blessed and sanctioned by God.

And We would like you to consider this:

"I am here on the Earth to become free."

The separation that began eons ago, created the energies and consciousness within which have enslaved human beings for as long as humanity has existed. Those who have rigorously done the spiritual work are at the end of your lives of struggle and bondage. You have returned to the Earth once again at this very powerful time, in order to achieve that final union with God that releases you from struggle and suffering and bondage.

And while you have served this Earth and served your fellow men and women in your past lives, and in this present incarnation, we remind you once again that your obligation is to fulfill yourself, and your task of opening to complete freedom.

Remember that there is no karma outside of you, it is within you. It lives within your emotional body. It lives within your psyche. So, you can free yourself, not through having experiences in outer reality that train you and purify you, but you can be freed of your karma within. And that is the holy and blessed work we do with you.

Your souls are being affected by what you are experiencing here. We are going to the deepest place within you.

This is a very powerful time on your planet energetically. On Earth you have created a world in which you could experience separation, in which you could experience what it would be like to be cut off from the love of God. Why you would want to experience that is a question you can ask yourself. The answer that your soul would tell you is: "Because you didn't know." And so, you wanted to know.

Although this experience has created pain and traumatized you in the whole of your life, it has also expanded you. And as the Angels of God, it is our task to reconnect you when you are ready to be reconnected.

There have been nonphysical beings who have had great power and influence on the planet, who have fed off your disconnected and separated energy. While it is difficult to accept that information, it is true.

What you have built through your experiences over all of this time on the planet is an energy of love through which God could enter in and effect change in the mass consciousness here.

So, at this tine you are receiving very powerful and new spiritual teachings, very powerful energy to utilize to liberate yourself.

There has not been sufficient openness in the past to receive on a mass level, the teaching that would completely free you. The teaching in its simplest form is that:

"You are one with God and God is love."

That is not a new teaching, and yet the false ego of man/woman has been so strong that it has been as if this teaching has never been heard, never been understood. You are one with God and God is love. That means all that you are is holy, all that you are is perfect, all that you are is absolutely lovable.

We are speaking to every soul on this planet on subconscious levels, so there is an awakening and a quickening happening in the collective energy. We are working to provide a path of liberation for everyone who is ready to be liberated.

And as I have said before, if there are souls who are not ready to be liberated they must live and grow elsewhere.

This planet is being saved, rescued, healed by God. So the inhabitants here must become compatible with the energy of God. Everyone on this planet must become loving. The truth is that everyone, every created being, is loving, but what must happen is that there must be a willingness to uncover the lovingness and let it be established as the Real Self.

It is a wonderful experience when this happens, and so you might ask: Why wouldn't everyone want to experience this? And, there is no logical answer to that question.

Remember that there has been an energy within that created the actual separation—and we call that energy through this channel, the false ego. And that part of the self is insane, so it cannot be understood logically.

I do not want you to dwell on these things. Rather I want you to concentrate on your own path of freedom and liberation, and know that no matter what you see happening around you on this planet; when you have cleared within, you are capable of creating for yourself—only loving experiences. That is the Law of Cause and Effect.

And know also, that our responsibility is to be there for every soul who wants healing. And prayer that comes from the heart is immediately answered, we are immediately sent to that human being to begin to work with the human being.

So, yes, this is a time of great change, but it is all change for the better; change that aligns life on this planet with the Will of Love.

Teachings from Michael 3

There are obviously many things going on on your planet simultaneously now. And as our brother Gabriel has said, you are responsible first and foremost for your own unification with your Higher Self, with the spirit of God within you. That is your obligation to yourself in this incarnation.

Many of you here have come to the Earth many times and have participated in many activities here. You have tried to reconstruct life here on outer levels and left various incarnations with a feeling of frustration, anger and grief because what you tried to accomplish did not hold in physical form. You neglected your own work of union, complete union with the spirit of God within yourself.

Many of you who will read this book have asked us before you were born into your lives in this present incarnation, to make sure we always brought you back to the Light, to a point of focus on healing and transformation in this incarnation. This we have been doing with you. We want to guide you now to a place of absolute, total and complete freedom.

You do not have a program or a frame of reference within your human mind regarding this. That it is even possible to experience this on the physical plane.

Yet, I tell you it is absolutely possible and it is the inevitable outcome of the work you are doing on yourself. You will reach this point of absolute, complete and total freedom if you stay with the work.

We understand quite clearly that this work can be very frustrating and you may feel that there are places within yourself that you simply cannot get past.

This is really an illusion and if you are really willing to go into the deepest level of emotional release you can absolutely free yourself of anything and everything that encumbers you in the free expression of your life and energy on the Earth.

We are working with you in and out of body state, where there is much planning and preparation going on. And you are being given information about what is to come on the Earth plane.

Tremendous energy is coming into the Earth now and this particular month is a time of tremendous energy. And as you have learned from the teaching you have been studying in this book, each soul who has been involved in life on the Earth is being given a choice now, is really being guided at unconscious levels. We are explaining to each soul that purification must occur now.

If there is a decision it is too much to take on the path of purification and liberation, you will see many entities electing to leave the planet and to process their consciousness and their energy elsewhere. They may then perhaps come back to the planet to begin to work again in a new form and a new incarnation.

So of course this means that you will need to process your feelings about physical death and you will need to feel within yourself that physical death is an illusion. Yet because your consciousness, your bodies have consciousness within them, you will feel naturally as you observe physical death occurring, a sense of grief.

Anytime you allow emotion to express freely through you, whatever the emotion is, it is healing and liberating for you and it brings you closer to the essence of love within you. It brings you closer to union with God within your own being.

Now while you will see entities leaving the Earth, you will see other entities being confronted with everything that they are holding within their emotional body that is presently manifesting in a loveless way. These souls have given us the decision that they want to stay on the Earth and work through their patterning in a physical body.

Each soul is given very deep counseling by us and any decision that is made about going or staying is come to in a painstaking and loving deliberate way with all variables being weighed.

But those of you who have done the work to free yourself and are becoming very powerful in light now will be given ministries. You will be given the task in the future of helping those souls who are electing to stay on the Earth and to work through their own process of healing and purification.

Your task will more and more be the task of channeling and sharing the light you have opened to.

You will see more of the projection or creation of spiritual truths in what you call your mass media, in films and television and books, in a way that is palatable and accessible to your general population on the Earth. This is a manifestation of the will of those who have elected to stay on the Earth to be given guidance and to be given what they need in order to heal and transform.

Those of you who are developing your gifts as healers and as mediums and as transmitters of light will be the ones who can actually facilitate the experience of opening to the Self of God within others.

I ask you now to take in a deep breath and allow the energy to move through you. Allow your emotions to process, as I continue by saying that if you have cleared within the emotional body, no matter what is happening on the Earth plane, you can live a life of free flowing joy and creativity.

This is what I mean when I say that there are and will be many things going on simultaneously. One entity will have the experience of their life on the planet as being heaven, a heaven that increases in its joy, while another entity occupying space on the very same planet will be having an experience of hell. That hell would only be what is held within the emotional body coming out into physical manifestation, or physical form as an opportunity for that particular soul to heal, to purify, to come into union with God.

I would like you to know that you have made great progress in liberating yourself. You are not to be afraid, either afraid of suffering that you will see in the future, or to be afraid that you will not be able to take on the responsibilities that will be given to you. No. As you come to balance within, everything that happens in your life will happen in the way of God. And by this I mean, as smoothly and as easily as possible, as a reflection of your unconditional loving acceptance of yourself.

Please let yourself open to understand that the world in and of itself is nothing, it is a blank slate. Your physical life, though, is simply outer reflections of what you are holding within.

As you move more and more into a consciousness of unconditional love and acceptance of yourself, there is a flow of joy and creativity in your life that reflects that inner consciousness. You will be in that flow no matter what is happening around you; this is the loving fairness of the universe. That you are responsible for your own energy for your own consciousness and when you are on the physical plane you are in physical space with other entities who are at varying levels of evolution but each entity is creating from wherever they are in consciousness.

But we cannot allow the planet to be destroyed by those who need to experience more of life in darkness and destruction. It is according to their own free will that they can do this but it cannot happen any longer on this planet.

I do not bring you this message to produce fear in you but it is our obligation to you, it is our task as your guides to keep you informed as to what is happening. It is not the will of God that any information be hidden from you.

Teachings from Michael 4

Be at peace. Be at peace. From a center of peace you can create according to your own heart's desire.

As I have mentioned before, great changes are taking place on the Earth plane now: a great sorting out is happening when certain souls are choosing to align completely with the Real Self of God within. Other souls are choosing to continue their development in other planes and on other planets. Other souls are choosing to leave the planet not because they want to create destructively, but because they want to take a rest from their processing and to join with us in the world of spirit; then to come back again in a new incarnation.

The next 20 years on this planet will be very powerful times of transformation. Those of you who are reading this are going to reap the benefits of the work you are doing right now.

Yes, the work is healing and evolving the emotional body. The work is releasing the minutest particles of consciousness of guilt and self rejection within, so you become a free being of God and you know your innocence. You feel it within your gut.

You may still be troubled by feelings of guilt within. Even though we say to you, you are the holy beloved innocent sons and daughters of God, there is a part of the self that refuses to believe and insists you are guilty. It insists you need to experience punishing situations, or to have a life in which you are denied your happiness. So we give you the message of God again, and each time you hear it, it goes to a deeper level of the self.

We understand very well how difficult the process of freeing yourself from guilt can be. But, as you join together in groups there is a great power of love that you generate and processing and healing can be speeded up immensely.

I would like you now to just focus on the teaching: "I am completely innocent—this is the word of God." *B r e a t h e* and feel the vibration that opens within you.

Now, we are very close in vibration to the Earth plane because the vibratory rate of the Earth plane has increased.

The non-physical beings that had great power on the Earth to keep you in darkness are being removed by the sheer force of the love that comes to this planet. This love is created by human beings through your having unconditional love and acceptance of yourself.

As you have unconditional love and acceptance of yourself you become completely invulnerable and there is then no outside force, whether a person or a non-physical being who can have any power over you, to hurt you, or to create anything in your life that is painful or that you do not want to have happen.

This is why we are teaching you over and over again that the goal of everything is to have unconditional love and acceptance of yourself; that is your self-protection. Guilt says, "I do not love myself, there is something wrong." This is why we will always guide you to the place where you are guilty and we will then guide you to invoke the presence of God in that place to release it.

If you do not have the openness to feel your guilt, it can be shown to you through your experiences on the Earth. If you are having experiences that are hurtful or you do not consciously want to have, you can know without any doubt that these experiences are a manifestation of guilt. **This is truth.** Guilt is released through your becoming conscious of it and then through your willingness to surrender it to God.

Now the energy is quite intense and we are working with you, as we are working with many human beings while you are in the sleep state. So you may find that your sleep patterns shift and change. I guide you to not resist the urge to sleep when you feel it. If it is possible, go ahead and sleep.

You may feel or go through times when you need to sleep for extended periods of time, this is because you are processing and you are being given counseling out of your body. You may then have periods of time where you require very little sleep and you are full of energy. Just leave yourself open for however your energy and your process manifests. It will always be organic and it will shift and change as the energy that comes to the Earth shifts and changes.

I guide you always to not hold the emotions in at all. If your life triggers you emotionally please let these emotions release.

When you go into meditation, and you formulate the thought that you want to have communion with your Higher Self and with God, then you receive an actual ray of energy from this plane of consciousness we call the Heart of God. This ray of energy effects a change within you. This is why in meditation you will feel at peace and often you will feel love afterwards or during it. There is an actual energetic change and process that is occurring.

We are encouraging you to go into meditation daily as much as possible. When you do so there is actually no limit, to how much you can grow. This is where your union with God takes place.

This is not a mental union that you simply read about or think about. You must experience it in your body. Understand that your body is part of the energy of God and is where you receive God when you are human and when you are on the Earth.

For those who take this seriously it is possible for your physical body to change radically and to always reflect the newness of yourself as your self opens to more and more love, as you open to the spirit of God more and more.

By doing this it is possible to overcome all sickness and to reach a state of consciousness where you never become ill. It is possible to reach a state of consciousness where you do not die in the conventional sense—instead death becomes a process that is quite conscious: you feel that you've had enough experience on the Earth and it is time to go elsewhere. There is no pain or trauma involved. You can reach a place where you are actually able to dematerialize this physical body and translate it into another plane of being.

As you ponder the reality of God who has created all of us and all that is, you will understand that as you come into a deep union with that power and you are limitless. Your union with that power comes through meditation. Since you are currently a physical being, that union comes through opening to it on the deepest level within your physical self.

When our brother Raphael says to you that it is possible for you to be completely free in this life on the Earth it is true. Do you see from what I am saying that it is true?

It is all up to you. How willing *are you* to become completely free in this life on Earth? How willing *are you* to allow the Spirit of God to fill you and merge with you?

While you are on Earth you may be going through a time of turbulence and chaos. You may also be awakening to great love and revelation. You can be in a center of peace and creativity and experiencing heaven on the Earth plane. For when you have cleared yourself you can no longer create anything for yourself other than the will of God—which is always your greatest joy, your greatest fulfillment, your greatest creativity.

Teachings from Michael 5

We bring you greetings from the Heart of God. Many are absorbing on a very deep level the teachings that we are bringing to man on the Earth at this time.

The teachings tell you it is absolutely possible for you to open to a state of complete freedom while you are on the Earth—to live in an energy of joy—to create heaven for yourself while you are on the Earth.

To open to this state your emotional body must be completely released from old trauma and must be completely released from the hold that guilt has had on it. As you work with these teachings you are gaining an understanding of the process of emotional release and how it is accomplished.

Our work as your guides and teachers is to constantly channel the energy of God into your energy field. This happens as you open in meditation.

Our work is to give you an understanding of what you are creating, how your life manifests and what the lessons that are to be learned are in any given situation or experience.

I have given you a synopsis of everything by giving you the teaching:

"I am here on Earth to learn the lesson of loving and accepting myself completely. I joyously open to learning that lesson. When I have learned that lesson, I will have no more problems and no more need for healing."

This is what I want you to focus on for a few moments: what it would be like to be absolutely free, with no more problems and no more need for healing. Just see that, feel that, and know that this is the Will of God for you.

Your spirit knows that state, but when you are incarnate in a body, the human consciousness that you form has never experienced that state but the spirit within you has and remembers it. As you are evolving through human life you are bringing the spirit and the body together, the spirit and the emotional body together as one.

In union with God, means there is no separation between the spiritual and the physical. All is one.

Now I wanted to speak to you about the plane of creativity and what happens when you are out of your body, when you are asleep.

As most of you know, your incarnations on the Earth are very well thought out and planned and guided. You receive counseling, you receive assistance, you receive healing, and you receive guidance in the world of spirit before you are born.

The parents you are born to, the country that you are born into, the race, religion—all have a purpose. They are teaching you about love and helping you to overcome the parts of the self that have developed a resistance to love, or are stuck in the trauma of the past; the past lifetimes on the Earth or the past in other realms. All of this must be healed so that you can go to another level where you can create freely, without struggle and without pain.

Yet the Earth plane is a plane of reality where you can be in that other level of consciousness, creating without struggle and without pain, while you are still in a physical body. So please let go of any notion that because you are in a physical body or because you are human or what you define as human must always mean you are limited or you must have trials and tribulations and struggle.

No, all of this is consciousness and when the consciousness does not hold guilt but only love, you are free, no matter what plane of existence you are living in.

Now we want you to understand that the counseling and the guidance does not only happen before you are born, but it is happening constantly while you are living your physical life.

You join with us in the world of spirit when you go into the sleep state, especially now because of the momentous changes that are happening on the Earth and within the human consciousness. We are touching in with you very deeply on a level of your consciousness that you are not aware of. But when sudden ideas or inspiration come to you, or you feel moved in certain directions that have a major effect in your life, know that you have been working within the plane of creativity. You have arranged an event, which then manifests on the physical plane in your physical life.

You are also studying in the world of spirit while you are living your life on the physical plane. And this is especially true for those who have surrendered your lives to the Will of God and who are on an active and aggressive spiritual path during your physical incarnation.

More and more you will not experience any sense of separation. You will feel our guidance and hear our guidance coming to you directly when you want to receive it consciously. You can go into a meditative state to receive it or it can come to you quite easily.

But, as I said to you before, when you feel the urge to sleep, if you can, do so. Please allow yourself to sleep and your sleep patterns will vary and change as the energy shifts on the Earth and as we have various needs to be with you and to work with you out of body.

Also, understand that your physical body will go through changes and you will feel, at times, the need to eat certain foods and to not eat certain foods; to ingest certain vitamins and minerals and to not ingest certain vitamins and minerals. It must all be organic and it must all come from your ability to listen to the intelligence of your spirit as it manifests through your body consciousness.

Now your deepest learning on the Earth plane comes through your relationships with each other. You each have many soul partners. Entities that you have been involved with on the Earth plane in various experiences and dramas. We feel from many human beings the need to join with others in love, in sexuality and in spiritual partnership.

We see also that this creates so much confusion and misunderstanding and pain on the Earth plane. While we are going to work through this channel on this subject in a workshop that comes to you in the near future we want to discuss it briefly here and now.

As you open to love in any relationship, you generate light. The love you experience with each other and for each other is light. It is the energy of God. It does feed and sustain our entire creation. Your major lessons on the Earth have to always do with love.

The truth that has been distorted and misunderstood on the Earth plane is that sexuality is the essence of the energy of God.

If there is a blockage in the flow of your sexual energy because of guilt within the psyche you bar yourself from having the spiritual partnership that you desire.

You also know and remember that when you are in a deep intimate relationship with another being you often create bliss. You often create the greatest joy and happiness that is possible and of course joy and happiness are attributes of God. They are part of the energy of God.

If then you feel within your psyche guilty and unworthy of receiving pleasure you will also bar yourself from having fulfilling spiritual partnership with another soul.

The work is always to ask that your ability to receive pleasure increase and increase and increase.

The reason why there tends to be so much upheaval in relationships once souls have joined together in loving sexual union is that they are not able to sustain the light that is generated. Their vehicles are not able to tolerate such pleasure and so the darkness enters in. The need to control, the need to abuse, the need to separate enters in. It is all guilt.

We wanted to give you this brief outline here because in the future many of you who desire it will join in spiritual partnership with other souls. This will not only feed your own ability to enjoy your life but it will be very important in service and in doing spiritual work on the planet.

For those who want to open to these kinds of relationships in a healthy joyous way, we are laying the ground work within you to make this possible.

But we want you to understand that always many plans are being outlined and created on the plane of consciousness that we call the plane of creativity. It is there where you decide to come together on the Earth plane with another soul.

Once you come together you do not really know each other in the personalities that you have as humans. Even if there is a soul connection it might not necessarily be conducive to a sustained relationship on the Earth plane, so you come together to find out. When there is a change in your location, your work, any major change is always first created on the plane of creativity where you enter into altered states of consciousness, and in the sleep state.

Teachings from Gabriel 1: Our purpose now is to give you back your power

There have been non-physical beings who have had great influence on this planet who have sought to keep humanities power away from humanity.

In this time of opening to God in a mass way that is occurring on the planet, our task as the angels of God is to help each and every soul to reclaim their power.

As you each are the holy beloved sons and daughters of God, in reality you are God.

When you open to your Real Self and come into union with it, which is the self of love, you can then truly know that you and the Father/Mother are one. Therefore you are God.

Your mind is the creator of your life experience. So our work is to undo the mass mental imprinting that has negatively influenced all human beings. We start by giving you an idea. You open, you listen to the words but you do not necessarily believe that the idea is true. But its seed has been planted in your mind and through your experience and through your focus on it, it then is revealed as being the truth.

Your mind is free to believe anything. But there is a fundamental objective truth and that truth is God, that truth is love. The only truth is love.

Now, I would like you to use your voice and say:
"The only truth is love."
Let us focus on love. If you understand that love is God, you can look at your creation and see and understand the nature of love and the nature of God. Love is life. The nature of God is always to sustain life.

That is the nature of love, to nurture, to nourish and to create. I would like you to work with that thought:
"The nature of love is to nurture, nourish and create."
Breathe and feel how that thought affects your energy field, your mind, your heart, your body.

You can then see how humanity collectively has Superimposed a whole reality over the essential nature of God and that reality is not true. The only truth is love.

Lack is not true. The only truth is love. Illness is not true. The only truth is love. Death is not true. The only truth is love. Suffering is not true. The only truth is love. Struggle is not true. The only truth is love.

B r e a t h e —and let the energy move through you, let yourself assimilate this information.

You may ask yourself: if these things, such as death, illness, lack and struggle are not true, then why do we experience them? It is because your mind is so powerful that you believe these things are true and therefore they become true, you create them.

But, above and below that is the fundamental truth, which is love. I want you to say these words:

**"I want my mind to be free and to accept only the
fundamental truth of love.
I am free."**

Teachings from Gabriel 2

We bring you greetings from the world of God and it is indeed our privilege to be able to, work with you once again.

I am Gabriel who speaks to you through this channel. We who are in the angelic realms are working with you to free your self from negativity so that you are able to live fully on the Earth plane in joy as you were created to live fully and in joy.

You are being given the task of letting go of previous notions and understandings as to who and what God is and what is possible for you to experience in your life on the Earth. For the teachings, the spiritual teachings that have come to the Earth in the past have been very much tainted by the collective self destructive will and have not had the fullness of truth within them. While they have had truth within them, it has not been the fullness of truth.

The fullness of truth tells you that you are meant to live in overflowing abundance. To be able to live in perfect health, to live without fear and to have the experience of physical death be a conscious choice and not an experience where one part of you chooses to die because it is so full of imbalance and pain and another part of you wants to continue to live.

The key to all of this, as you understand through the work that has been given through this channel and which you have explored in previous classes is the healing and evolution of the emotional body.

I urge you to work with the teaching in the book *Right Use of Will*. There is a very powerful and important sentence in that teaching which tells you that all of manifested existence has had the goal of self-acceptance.

Last week in this class my brother Michael gave you the affirmation that the lesson you are learning on the Earth plane is to love yourself. You said you willingly and joyously open to learning that lesson.

I would like to begin our meditation by having you focus on that once again:

"The lesson I am learning on the Earth is to love myself.
I joyously open to learning that lesson."

Now, I would like you to pay close attention to any shifts that occur in your energy as you work with that thought. "The lesson I am learning on the Earth plane is to love myself. I joyously open to learning that lesson." If you felt any resistance it comes from a feeling of being unworthy. The feeling of not feeling worthy is guilt.

Guilt is unreasonable. It is insane and it has no reason to be, it has no reason to exist. And yet each human entity has tremendous guilt that is for the most part unconscious.

Your traditional religions have fostered that guilt and it has become associated in the human psyche with God. It is the opposite of what is true.

I would like you to simply give yourself the thought: **"My guilt is unreasonable and it is the opposite of God."**

In giving yourself that thought you should feel within your body and your consciousness a sense of calm and peace.

Now what I would like to do is to give you an outline as to how to work on the self.

When any human being calls out for help and guidance from God, which is what prayer is, we who are the angels of God are sent to serve that human. What we do is work with your consciousness and with your auric field. As you become more and more open you feel our presence with you.

Your life is truly a psychological process, so our guidance and help comes through helping you to see and know and understand your own psyches, your own consciousness.

In working on yourself when you meditate you are drawing in the energy of God, the energy of the life force. This activates your consciousness and it activates your emotional body, so you will start to manifest whatever you are holding within your emotional body and this might happen rather quickly.

This is a great process of teaching you. You need only look at what your life is manifesting in order to learn your lessons and to see your truth.

You are created to experience the fullness, the joy, the magnificence of life, and certainly not to be stuck or to suffer pain and hardship. But if the emotional body has accumulated aspects of consciousness that create suffering or hardship, it is these aspects of the self that it is our task to release from you.

Your task is to respond to what you are manifesting. I will give you an example. Perhaps you are manifesting being fired from a job on the Earth plane or you are manifesting not having enough money to sustain your life. In working on yourself, you would allow yourself to really feel the feelings triggered within you.

In your own space, where you have privacy and where you are safe, you would allow yourself to express those feelings, you would let them come through the voice in whatever way they needed to come in the most dynamic way possible. You would let your body express the feeling and in that way you would be moving the pattern out of your energy field. We would be with you, channeling into your energy field the Light of God. That is the very *active* process of working on yourself.

Working on yourself also includes a contemplative process which you are becoming familiar with in this class in which you listen for our voice and we guide you into an intellectual understanding of your lessons and yourself.

But as you work with us daily you do indeed become freer and freer and more and more in union with God.

Now, as we have said, the planet Earth will not be allowed to be destroyed. Humanity will not be allowed to physically destroy this planet. The heart of God is sending tremendous love to this planet for the purpose of healing the consciousness here.

Many things are manifesting because the collective emotional body is being activated. As we said previously, what will occur is that souls who are not actively working to open to love, to open to God, to open to healing will not be able to vibrationally sustain their lives here. They will need to live in other planes of existence; on other planets in order to fulfill their evolutionary process.

The Earth will become a place of development for souls who truly want to align with the will of love.

Most human beings do not understand what is occurring now and the manifestations are quite tragic and extreme. This is simply the out picturing of what the collective and individual emotional body is holding.

We want to work with you to help clear any imbalance you are holding so that you can manifest peace and joy and fulfillment in your life on the Earth.

This is open to all manifested spirits, but not all manifested spirits are willing to do the work involved to clear the self, nor are they even desirous of doing so. There is a desire on the part of some manifested spirits to stay in the experience of negativity and pain, even if they consciously do not admit this or acknowledge that it is still their will and desire.

Question: "Can we help those who are not open, such as loved ones and family?"

Answer: "That is a very wonderful question and the answer is you can only help souls who want to be helped. It is that simple. Each soul will come to the point where they do want to be helped.... not necessarily in this lifetime or in this experience. There does come a point in the evolution of every soul where they have had enough of pain and suffering and negativity and then are open to being helped. It is always helpful, though, to pray for others, to send them the energy of love. That energy can open them and activate the memory of God within them."

Question: "When we do a movement or emotional release, why do we have to go back again and again, why isn't once enough?"

Answer: "That is also a very excellent question. There are layers upon layers of trauma in the emotional body as well as resistance and an energy of fear within the emotional body that cannot take in the fullness of light all at once.

If you visualize someone who has been in darkness for a long period of time and if they open the door and light was coming through the door, they would shield their eyes and be blinded by it and would not be able to live within it. This is what the darkness within the emotional Body is like and so it must be approached a little at a time, in order to get used to living in the light. That is why emotional release or emotional movement is an ongoing process."

Question: "Because of the fear we have part of ourselves in denial and that makes it impossible to do this on a conscious level. You have to wait for the emotion. Why is this?"

Answer: "This is something that we monitor and work with you on. We help you to bring up what you can work with, to bring up aspects of consciousness that would naturally or normally be in a state of denial or unconsciousness. When you give us permission to work with you, we understand perfectly your process, your rhythm and how you can best heal. Each soul, who really is serious about healing and transformation, receives so much help and guidance from us."

Question: "Could you give a more specific example about working on yourself in this process?"

Answer: "First of all, you would need to be present in your life experience, to accept that your life experience is reflecting to you what you are holding within. Perhaps you are experiencing repeated rejection by others. What we would do then in your meditation is guide you into your childhood in which you experienced the same kind of rejection from one of your parents to show you how that locked into your emotional body.

We encourage you to release the feelings. If that rejection, that initial rejection caused you to feel angry but you felt that it was wrong to express the anger, we would encourage you to yell, to strike out in a way that does not harm yourself or anyone else but through your own process in privacy. That way you would release the initial pattern of rejection. We would also give you a teaching of truth about yourself, such as, "You are completely loved, lovable, and acceptable," and that is then how you would lift the pattern from your energy field You would find that you would not repeat the pattern of rejection in your adult life."

Question: "Can we release specific issues that we are working on in this lifetime?"

Answer: "Yes you can. If you are willing and you do the work and you follow the guidance you can certainly release any issue in this lifetime."

Question: "Is our purpose to become light bodies? Is the guidance I've been getting to take care of the body very important?"

Answer: "Yes. The physical body is simply the out picturing or the form that the inner consciousness takes. As you take care of the inner self, your physical body will naturally come into alignment.

Now, of course, there are things you can do specifically for the physical body to help it come into alignment but the real work is with the inner consciousness and with receiving light from the heart of God.

When you say the goal is to become light bodied, this is true. If it is possible for the human body to become so evolved, if the inner consciousness becomes so evolved it does become a light body. In that way the body itself can simply translate into other realms of being.

You have heard of masters who have been able to do this. Of course the one example you all are familiar with is the man Jesus. This is really the inheritance of all humanity, the ability to do this. But what we see as a more achievable goal for this particular time is the goal of having physical death be a conscious choice rather than something that occurs because there is a split within."

Question: "Are you saying that we don't have to die?"

Answer: "I am saying that it can become a process in which you die or you shed your body simply because you desire to, because you have had enough experience with it on the Earth."

Meditation from Gabriel

I am Gabriel and I am sent to the Earth from the Father-Mother because so many souls have prayed and asked for healing and enlightenment.

I want to discuss with you the work you are doing, in freeing the emotional body, freeing the will.

It is very important for you to understand the Earth, up until this point has been almost smothered by an energy which is counter to life, and counter to love. It has not allowed the Will within individuals to be free—and to receive the nourishment of the light from God needed for life to be lived, manifested, and sustained according to the will of God.

So many human beings are confused about who and what God is. They have looked to and worshipped an image, an entity and energy that is truly not God.

The presence of God—the very real and powerful presence of God is on the Earth right now. It is affecting the energy, the inner being, and the inner selves of absolutely every human being on the planet.

This is causing a major uprising in consciousness, and a major uprising in groups, in individuals, and a feeling within of needing to be free and demanding freedom. This is creating for you a very deep societal restructuring.

We are training those of you who have asked to be trained, and who are open to receiving the light of God to be free.

You can only be free when you have healed your own will, your own emotional body, and when you have come into deep connection and relationship within your body, within your mind, within your heart with God the Father—Mother of all life.

You then begin to experience the truth that you are not at all to be limited.

I work with a great fellowship of beings who have the task of guiding, opening, healing human beings who want to grow, and who want to unify with the energy of God, and with their own Spirits. We prepare your mind and your body and your heart for this receptivity.

Most of you reading this book are opening to a very tangible experience of the energy and intelligence of God within your bodies.

You have been told that this is the inheritance of all humanity, that this will be the new way of life on the Earth plane and this is the truth. Life will come to a place where it will be impossible for the self to be sustained without this deep connection to the spirit within the body.

I would like to guide you in a meditation with ideas that you have heard before, but I want you to open your heart and your mind to nurture these ideas, and you will feel a shift created within.

The first idea is:

"God is unconditional love."

Let yourself say that within:

"God is unconditional Love. God loves me unconditionally. Everything about me is perfect and right. Everything about me is perfect and right. I was created to live in abundance. I was

created to live in abundance. I do not have to struggle and have hardship and problems.

I do not have to struggle and have hardship and problems. Hardship and problems are not the will of God for me. Freedom is the will of God for me. I do not ever have to be sick or physically limited in any way. I do not have to be sick or physically limited in any way.

Perfect health is the will of God for me. My life on the Earth is supposed to be incredibly joyous. My life on the Earth is supposed to be incredibly joyous. A life of joy is the will of God for me."

Now, if you are sufficiently sensitive, you may feel beings of light surrounding you and working with your energy. We would like you to become as surrendered as possible, as if you were going to go to sleep—and we will open the centers of light within your body, and this will happen in the silence.

Part 4

From the Angels of Healing and Transformation

Introduction

The following teachings were given through channeled sessions of "The Spiritual Psychic Development Class" I teach at the "First Universal Spiritual Church of New York City. The source of the channeling, are the Angels of Healing and Transformation.

We are never alone. God's help is ever present. When we sincerely pray from our heart and soul we are sent angels to minister to us and help us.

I believe the real purpose of life on the Earth is the transformation of self, the healing and transformation of what these teachings call the false ego.

In order for this to be accomplished we need help. The help comes from God through the angels of healing and transformation.

When we meditate, they come to us and channel spiritual energy into our body through our chakras/energy centers.

They inspire our thoughts in such a way that we are guided to the fulfillment of our purpose on the planet.

Their task is to bring us truth; the truth about ourselves, our lives, and about Life itself.

Whenever I do a private reading or teach a class or workshop the angels of healing and transformation are supplying the energy and information given.

The following talks are of general interest to persons on a spiritual path of inner transformation. Open to and enjoy the teachings.

"Ask and ye shall receive."

Rev. Daniel Neusom

The Urge Toward God

We bring to you our greetings and our blessings from the world of reality. Our hearts at this time are filled with joy at seeing your growth and development

You must understand fully and completely that your joining together is no accident. The cry within the heart that you have felt is a sign from your soul, a sign from your eternal self that it is time to return home.

By the statement "It is time to return home" we mean it is time to return to a consciousness of God. A consciousness of God is a consciousness of wholeness and balance.

In this class we have spoken of the separation, the fall, the entrapment in matter. We want you to understand that separation has resulted in the present state of mankind's consciousness, being entrapped in a belief the body is all there is to life, and that life ends with the death of the body; that the mind, the human mind is the ruler of all.

Yet, within the consciousness that humanity presently lives within, there is still the memory of God. This memory acts as a fire within. It acts as an urge toward happiness. Yet, human beings discover that happiness is really not found through acquiring wealth or power on the Earth, happiness is not found through acquiring material possessions, happiness is not found through overpowering one-another. This call or this urge toward happiness is a distorted urge toward union with God. It is the urge to find love.

As you who are in this room are beginning to discover, the love that mankind seeks is the love of the Real Self, the Eternal Self, the Self of God within. This Self as you are beginning to experience, is not a concept, but it is a real and powerful living force that you can touch and activate within yourself when you call for it, when you are ready to receive it.

The readiness to receive this force which is in truth the Light of God, only comes after there has been enough experience in relating and experiencing on the Earth out of the false ego self.

So you have come to this point after many, many prior life experiences in relating to the Earth and to other human beings through the false ego self.

The learning in the false ego self is of course the learning of love and compassion.

When you have discovered what is created through the experience of the false ego self, and its guilt and its urge to destroy; when you have been on both ends of that urge to destroy, the destroyer and the one destroyed, a feeling of love and compassion opens up within. There is a feeling of union with all humanity.

You do not see yourself as being separated. You let go of the need to judge others because of their race or their sex, or their sexual orientation or their religion, all of the things that seem to be barriers for human beings as they attempt to relate to each other.

Once there has been the experience of taking on many different roles, many different places within the structure of different cultures, there is an understanding that you are one, that humanity is in truth one, the beloved son/daughter of God; God's beloved offspring. Humanity in its collective being is one. When this is truly experienced then life on the Earth can evolve into a new experience. The new experience comes from a new consciousness.

You understand very well the false ego consciousness as we have talked about it over and over again. The new consciousness is the consciousness of God, the consciousness of love.

In this consciousness you have opened to that living force we speak of. Once that living force unites with your mind and with your body, you come into balance. The process of coming into balance is often wrought with upheaval or deep times when you feel yourself out of balance.

Understand always, that it is never a question of what is happening to you in your physical life, because all imbalance is within your own consciousness.

When you surrender to God, when you call out for God to dwell within you, when you open to this consciousness that we are speaking of, all of the imbalances within are seemingly exaggerated. This is so you can fully see them and understand them and then choose to perceive yourself, your world, your life, in a different way.

Your consciousness can never shift or change or heal until you fully understand it and make the choice to be in a different state of consciousness.

Along this path you will also have a deep experience of your emotional body. All of the reactions you have had in your life on Earth in prior lives come up for your release.

You must understand that this emotional release is a process in which the Light of God descends more and more into your aura. That Light manifests as the heart of God, and that heart which is an actual pulsating energy absorbs the pain of your traumatic experiences and gives you the feeling of being renewed. **This is how healing is accomplished.**

Always know that no matter what you are experiencing, when you call out to God, to the Holy Spirit of God, there is a part of God that is absorbing your emotional trauma, guiding you and healing your energy. This guidance may manifest as insights that come into your own consciousness through your connection with your guides, or it may come through your guides steering you to people, to books or teachings that will stimulate the transformation you are seeking. Whenever you call out you are heard and you are responded to.

The only limitation to the depth of healing and transformation that you experience is an unwillingness to face the deeper levels of the self and to feel the emotions that those levels of the self hold. The unwillingness is always based on a fear that the self is evil at root. This is not true. Your essence is love.

Evil manifests as love that has become so distorted and that is so in pain that it cannot manifest in a loving way. So, no matter what you discover within yourself, always keep going. No matter how angry you have become at other human beings, no matter how frustrated you may feel about your circumstances or your life, those feelings must be expressed and acknowledged, but they are *not* who you really are. Your essence is love.

You are now experiencing an evolution into this new consciousness, but most human beings are not so spiritually aware. They feel a shift within themselves, or a desire for peace, and they observe that great physical changes are taking place on the Earth. But while they observe the new maturity that is collectively coming to humanity, they do not understand exactly what is happening.

You who are able to directly access the light and consciousness of spirit are actually bringing into the Earth plane, the light which affects the evolution and healing of mankind collectively. This is because you are the sons and daughters who were first and whose return is first.

We want you to focus now on your own life and experiences. For the places where you are fulfilled and at peace where your light flows and creates for you your heart's desire, let yourself say thank you. And for the places where you are not at peace, let us work to heal.

See very clearly where there is discord, unhappiness, or lack in your life. And see how this connects to a feeling within that a part of you is not acceptable or not worthy of being loved. See how it connects to a feeling of being undeserving. See how it connects to a feeling of shame or badness. Recognize this as being guilt; guilt based on experiences you have had or illusions you believe to be true.

Ask now to experience a shift within yourself. Ask to be able to perceive yourself completely in love. And, whatever the situation, whatever the problem, turn it over to the Holy Spirit of God now, that it may be corrected and healed. Give that spirit permission to work through this situation, this feeling, this problem, whatever it is.

Question: "When I ask for something to be healed, is it done?"

Guide: Yes. When you ask for healing, the first thing that happens is that you become aware of your creative power, how you have created the situation. You become aware of your error or the part of yourself that is manifesting guilt.

You become fully conscious of it. And as this happens you will often have an emotional recognition of this and an emotional experience related to the situation.

You are always to allow this to express through you and freely because this is how your magnetic center or the part of the self that manifests experience, how it clears itself, through your emotions.

Then when you have fully understood the workings in your own consciousness that created the imbalance, you are ready to release it. Then what happens is what we call through this channel, a miracle, inasmuch as the light of God takes over and it is lifted from you, whatever it is. That is the final stage of the healing process. It is when the aspect of self that is not in truth opens and receives light and the situation, whether it is an outer experience or an inner experience is healed.

Question: "Can you explain what karma is?"

Guide: "Karma is not the experience of being punished for what you have done in past lives. Karma is your own consciousness, if you understand what we say about the fall or the separation as being the separation from the expression of love. Your karma is how that has manifested for you in your past lives, so that when you are born, when you begin a new incarnation, encoded in your energy field is the consciousness, an amalgamation of the consciousness that you have left behind in the Earth's energy field in your prior lives. That is your karma.

"Your karma will manifest in the parents that you are born to and in the experiences of your early childhood. Those experiences bring into clear focus the places within your soul that you need to balance in a life, that you need to bring back into lovingness.

"You must always understand that your karma is not something that is set and not something that you have no control over. Once you recognize that your karma is simply your own consciousness, then the work becomes bringing your consciousness back into love through the process that we describe.

"When you do this your physical life changes and you are not bound by karma. Your karma is always expressing what needs to be balanced within."

You can expect to see more great changes on the Earth. These changes are really the pull toward balance and love. Even though they may express in a difficult way, you will see the underlying thread is that more love is coming to the Earth. More balance is coming to the human consciousness.

The places within the human consciousness that have expressed for centuries in a state of imbalance will often manifest as an energy of anger or destructiveness. This is part of the process as a whole. If you can relate this to your own personal process you will see that that is part of the coming into balance.

The places that are out of balance become enlightened or seem to have a spotlight focused on them. This you will see happening collectively. Then there will be the desire to change, to heal. This will be expressed collectively. Finally, the whole experience of life is transformed and can then begin to express from a core of love.

So, that all of the many imbalances which have been part of human consciousness and the expression of life on this plane are and will be healed through each succeeding generation.

You will each be able to come into more and more personal happiness and balance. This will separate you in experience from many of your brothers and sisters. They will not really be able to understand why you are the way you are or why your life expresses in the way that it expresses.

We urge you to relate to your brothers and sisters from openness, perceiving within your own heart who is open to hearing and understanding your truth and experience and letting yourself share that truth and experience. This can inspire; can open another human being to come to a path of light, a path of healing, a path of transformation.

You will all recognize that you are teachers on this planet, even if you do not actually become spiritual teachers. It is through your life and through your relationships that you will teach your brothers and sisters, simply through being who you are.

Be not ashamed of the light within you. Be not ashamed of the love within you. Be not ashamed of the freedom that you will express more and more, the freedom that comes from unconditional self-acceptance and love. Let yourself live that freedom without apology; knowing that that is your inheritance and it is your creator's will for you.

We thank you very much for your efforts at growth, for those efforts influence life in many planes of existence.

We are with you always to serve you, to guide you, to help you to understand your experience and to help you to come into union with God within your own body and your own energy fields.

Be blessed and be in God forever.

Channeled Healing Service

The Heart of God

We bring to you our greetings from the Heart of God, a plane or field of energy that embraces this planet now and through and from which the will of God can be known and can be manifest on this planet.

God is to human beings, a mysterious and unknown force. As you look about you in your world, you see that there is order, you see the miraculous forms that life manifests through and so you know that there is some force, some intelligence that has created all that is and sustains all that is.

You recognize yourself as being conscious, as having self consciousness, yet you do not know how you came to be or where you came from, you do not know where the center of life is, the center of being is. That center of being is God and in essence that center of being is unknowable but it is very important for you to understand that that center of being sends out rays of light which seek to nourish and guide and help all that it has created.

When you pray,when you ask for healing, guidance and help,what you are doing is opening yourself for guidance, for help, for love from God. That ray of love is not an amorphous intangible thing, that ray of love is an energetic, intelligent aspect of consciousness or Light which can embrace you and which can guide you and give you insight and which has the power to transform your consciousness and activate a process in which the aspects of your self or your consciousness which are non-moving begin to move, begin to become enlightened, begin to receive the nourishment that they are crying out for, that they need in order to live.

Your pain, your struggle, your problems, these are all manifestations of a part of your energy, a part of your consciousness a part of your being crying out to receive nourishment. That nourishment is the love of God.

Opening to the Light of God

We bring to you our greetings and our blessings from the world of God. You now are being touched by the heart of God. And through this energy of love which you are being given because you have asked to receive it, you will become more and more capable of transforming yourself and your life.

We would like to talk to you about what is happening on your planet at this tine.

For many eons the Earth has been a planet which has not been open or able to receive the degree of light necessary for there to be balance and wholeness within the life manifesting upon it. The life of the sentient beings that are presently manifested on the Earth and most especially for those of you who are human entities has greatly influenced the energy field of the Earth.

Now the Earth's energy field is very essential to this entire creation. The Earth itself is very essential to this entire creation and so there is a great healing that is coming to the planet through the being of God releasing more and more light into the planet's own energy field. Those of you who are now living on the Earth are feeling and will continue to feel the effects of this light, which comes to the Earth.

Now, of course, light is love. Light is the Creator. Light sustains life itself. But where there is blockage or non-moving energy, light can be experienced as being painful.

We have guided this channel to teach and speak about the healing of guilt and self-hatred. Within the human energy field those are the two currents that block the free flow of light from the center of the being of God into the human energy field.

We want you to understand that all life is deeply connected and manifests from this great nebulous of intelligent energy and consciousness that you know as God.

So that in the purification of the planet what you will experience personally is a need to release any and all of your denials. By this we mean the parts of the self that you are not conscious of but which have nonetheless been creators for you will come up into your consciousness to help you to better understand yourself and your life situation.

For most human entities the currents of guilt and self-hatred are unconscious currents. But as you open to light, as you surrender more and more to the will of God, you become quite conscious of parts of yourself that were hidden which lay within the emotional body which were created from past life experiences. What you will experience is a kind of volcanic activity in the emotional body. You become conscious also of energies of deep grief then a piercing of the heart. This piercing of the heart we speak of is the opening of the heart where the feelings that have been suppressed for many, many lives come up and you feel them and they must be released freely.

They will often seem extreme and irrational but you must always understand there is a part of yourself that has been blocked and inactivated for eons of time that is crying out for healing and for realignment. As the planet itself receives this light it must bring every aspect of consciousness on the planet into balance.

This of course creates many upheavals in your world and we want you to not be afraid. Many people who are psychics or prophets have been predicting the end of the world or doomsday or disaster that would obliterate life on this planet. We want you to know this cannot and will not happen, because this planet is too important for the balance of the entire creation. We would like you to not focus on those theories, or those predictions, or that understanding of what is happening, but rather to continue to focus on healing yourself and bringing your own life into balance.

When you surrender to the will of God and to the will of the Higher Self, what you are doing is giving God permission to give to you the light you need to be healthy and nourished sufficiently on this planet. This light is given to you through your chakras, through the energy centers which are in the human body and which are connected to various layers of the aura.

You will all begin to feel more and more, this light, this Shakti, this prana, flowing through you. You will change and your relationships with others will change. Those who are not electing to align with the higher purpose of healing, and balancing, and opening to enlightenment, and are choosing to remain within the confines of the false ego self and the old way of being, you will find that you will be very conflicted with those people. There will be a need to really observe your own false egos at work. To always understand what is happening in any relationship, that when you are in conflict, to shift gears so you focus in the awareness and the consciousness of the higher self and so your false ego does not get into a battle with the false ego of another. In this way, you can transform your relationships. You must constantly pray and ask for the ability to exercise or live within the consciousness of forgiveness and understanding and compassion.

When you are in relationships in which you are negated, or feel another person's anger projected onto you, you will have to weigh within your heart whether to remain in the relationship, whether there is a possibility for healing the relationship on the Earth plane. Your heart will tell you this. And, if there is not, if there is no willingness on the part of the other person to grow and to change and to evolve, then you must, without guilt, let go of the relationship.

The energy that is coming to this planet will affect the heart chakra of everyone more and more. So people who have felt powerless, who have been willing to let others control their lives, to let governments that are not heart-conscious governments control their activities, the human activities on the planet, these people will feel within themselves, an inability to continue. They will feel a surge of power, so that many governments will change and will more and more reflect heart consciousness.

Those of you who are mystics, who are actually able to open to receiving and channeling the energy of God through your energy field and into the planet, are serving a very great purpose. You are keeping the balance on the planet and you are helping it to heal and evolve.

Every aspect of denial or pain or blockage that you heal within yourself is an opening of love that feeds life on this planet itself.

Question: "How do you know whether or not you should end a relationship?"

Guide: "If you feel that you are repeatedly being abused and frustrated and you have prayed for healing and see no change and you have observed your part, your false ego at work, and you have made a change in your own approach to the relationship and you still are receiving abuse or negation, then that is when you know it is time to let go of it, when the relationship continually pulls you down."

Question: "When it sucks energy from you?"

Guide: "Yes."

Question: "You mentioned the word rage. In what area would that be comfortable?"

Guide: "Rage is anger that has been suppressed or negated or denied so that it becomes exaggerated. When you have received repeated abuse or negation in prior lives and in this life, there is something in the root chakra or the survival chakra that recognizes that the loving response to receiving abuse or negation is anger. Not a destructive anger toward those who are projecting their self hatred and anger onto you but an anger which protects you from harm, an anger which is the precious love of the self."

"So when we speak of rage, as this light enters into your energy field, if you have denied emotions, if you have denied anger, anger that has not moved for a long time, it will be exaggerated, it will manifest as rage."

"Rage is to be released in a place of privacy and safety where you cannot harm yourself and others. You are to let the rage release through movement and through sound, through your body until you feel an opening in the energy field until you feel that this suppressed ball of rage has opened and has come into a kind of balance. The healing of rage is a long process from your perspective but in truth it really is not a long process."

Teaching on Guilt

Your whole world is a reflection of the guilt you and other human beings feel within your souls. Most of you are unaware that this is the truth.

At this time on the Earth, we are sending our light here as we never have been able to before. For although there is still tremendous guilt within your consciousnesses, you have evolved to a place of love where we can be received.

This new era that you are moving into necessitates that you understand that you have built a whole world, a whole civilization, a whole way of life on a lie—the belief that you are guilty. This guilt originated with the initial separation from love that happened before the human being and the human consciousness came into being or existence.

The human consciousness as it is now, is a manifestation of guilt, of being separated from love, and being at war within the self.

Because the Spirit is love, and cannot be extinguished, it has always been with you. Yet the layers of guilt that the false ego has taken on, because of the separation and because of all the cruel, vicious, hostile acts that have been experienced on the Earth, has created this war within the self of guilt versus love.

Guilt opposes the evolution and expression of love, and as each human being receives our light and love in a mystical way, within the body through the soul, the belief in guilt is eradicated—it is wiped away through the experience of God, through the miracle.

When you experience God, you do experience your own innocence, and your own pure love, and the greatest teaching that this experience gives you—is that guilt is unreal, and does not exist.

If you doubt what we are teaching about guilt, we ask you to question yourself: "Why is it so difficult for you to fully and completely love yourself?" "Why do you struggle so much with yourself?" "Why do you have such difficulty achieving and maintaining happiness, and health and abundance and peace?"

It is the force of guilt within you. You believe in it and give it power. We will give you a miracle now. The miracle will be your knowledge that by believing in guilt and giving it power, you have believed in nothing and given it power.

We give you now our peace, our blessing and our love.

Prayer for the Healing of Guilt

I am the Holy Spirit within me. I am the real self within me. I am the love within me. Anything else I believe I am is false. And the miracle I ask for is the absolute knowledge and experience of this. I leave my self open for it. I surrender my fear. I surrender my guilt. I surrender the will of my false self to the Heart of God within me.

Amen

The Healing of Fear and Lovelessness Within

We bring you greetings and blessings from the heart of God.

As you continue to vibrate and move within your emotional body, you reach while you are on the Earth plane, the realm of God.

In that realm, you experience yourself as being masters. This means that the Earth no longer contains energies or elements, or forms that cause you to be afraid.

The source of all fear is always within your consciousness as the memories of what you have experienced in the past, whether it is in this life or in others, that has created suffering for you. That is the source of all fear.

The experiences that you have had where you have suffered have been experiences that have taken place because you have not had your full power with you.

Man on the Earth has not had the full power of God in manifestation through the life experienced within the body as a human being.

In this new era that has already begun, the experience of being in the body will be radically different, and it will not be the human experience that has been known in the past.

You understand very fully that God is love, but you must prepare your self to receive God and to receive your full power. This preparation of the self is the healing of all lovelessness within.

We speak here of the healing of fear and the healing of lovelessness within.

We would have you now work with the intelligence and energy of God, which is vibrating within you now asking:

"Dear God, expose to me now the fear that I am ready to work through and release."

And allow yourself to see images and hear information.

As you examine and work with this fear, you have probably been given a scene or information regarding something that has happened to you in the past that was painful whether it was the past from this life or another. The conclusion that is drawn within your emotional body then is that life is painful and is something that you must fear and defend yourself against.

The conclusion that is drawn within your emotional body is that people will hurt me, so I must defend myself.

Can you see how that cuts off your energy?

As we go back to the scene, the source of your fear, where the conclusion was drawn, ask yourself: How did I feel about myself at the time of this painful experience that started my belief in fear?

You will find that you were not vibrating in full love and acceptance of yourself. That is what left you open to the painful experience that created the belief in fear.

That is the separation, not vibrating in full love and acceptance of the self. That is guilt, not vibrating in full love and acceptance of the self.

You can see that the thought system of your world is based on guilt. Guilt blocks out love—the love of God, the light of God.

The cells within your body have all of the information you need to know to understand yourself, and the journey you have made in manifestation. The cells within your body have learned to reject life.

The teachings we bring to the Earth plane now are to reach the intelligence within the cells of your body, so that you fully open to life. That is how your emotional body is healed, and your lost will is recovered.

Listen now, to your body, and let your body tell you how it feels about you. Your body can speak to you. Within the presence of God/Creator here, your body will tell you the truth, and how it feels about you.

If your body has told you it loves you absolutely and unconditionally, then know you are fully aligned with the will and heart of God. If your body has exposed any rejection of you, know it is your task, now, to invoke the presence of God to bring healing.

The Process of Purification

We give you our blessing and we bring you greetings from the Heart of God.

There is great light, there is great power, there is great love entering the energy field of the Earth right now, and entering into the energy fields of all human beings who are presently experiencing and expressing life on the planet.

This energy is love, and yet, if the self/the soul is not purified, this energy moving through it can bring into manifestation experiences that seem unloving or cruel.

We have worked very strongly with this group in opening you to receiving an understanding of the emotional body or the magnetic center. This is the place within your soul where you hold your memories from past lives, where you hold your beliefs about reality, where you hold all of the experiences that have created what you have known in manifestation. You hold all of the consciousness that has created what you have experienced in manifestation.

As the light of God floods this planet it seems to enter into all of the manifesting forms of life on the planet. If there is consciousness within the emotional body that is distorted or fear-based or guilt-based, the light coming towards the emotional body will bring into manifestation whatever the consciousness is that the emotional body is holding.

This is what can create the suffering that seems to happen to people who are innocent and to people who are trying as best they can to manifest a life of love.

It is what can make it seem that there is no God of love who answers the call for help and healing. This is why we must bring this understanding that there is indeed a God of love, who wants to heal and love everything it has created, but the healing process is a process of freeing the emotional body from any unloving consciousness that it is holding.

The goal, as you all know, is to reach a place within yourself where you have absolute, unconditional love for every aspect of your self. This means absolute and unconditional love and acceptance for your body, love and acceptance of your sexuality, of your past lives, of your present life—of everything.

The destructive force within the human consciousness, as we have said before, has always been guilt. Guilt not as a feeling of remorse for loveless acts created in the past, but guilt as a feeling that there is part of the self that is not acceptable, and not worthy of love.

As we have said before, this guilt really began with the beginning of life in the body on the Earth plane. It is a product of the feeling that it is/was evil, wrong, or bad to willingly turn away from love, and to begin to experiment with life in the world of matter. This is a deep existential misunderstanding within the soul that most human beings are not even conscious of.

Most human beings are not conscious of the role that guilt has played in their lives. It is healing to bring this into an awareness—and to have the light of God release it from the soul, so that life can manifest in freedom as it was meant to be, and as is the will of God.

When life manifests in freedom, it means that there is no death, there is no sickness, there is no lack, there is no want, there is no hunger. It means everything that is needed for life to manifest in health and abundance is instantly within the self, and can manifest outwardly.

This is in truth the nature and will of God. If you think about this, you will see that this is not occurring on the Earth plane. So, there must be some force which blocks the will of God. That force, as we have said before, is guilt—and guilt is and must be lifted from the energy field of man/woman and from the Earth.

This is the great teaching that Jesus came to the Earth to deliver to humanity. It is the great teaching he brings to humanity now through the spiritual path of *"A Course in Miracles"*—that the holy beloved son of God is guiltless, and the separation, in truth, has never occurred.

If there are any unhealed places within your emotional body right now, you can rest assured you will become very aware of what they are. Your outer life will show you this.

We want to give you advice and counseling in how to process the various things that may occur on your path at this time. Become very, very sensitive to your inner feelings. Any experience of pain or discomfort or unease, is to be explored. It is a signal that God is calling you to pay attention to something that is going on within yourself.

We have said many times before it is very essential to have a daily practice of meditation and prayer, and inner listening, so that as you become aware of any sort of discomfort or pain or uneasiness. You can go directly into your inner temple and receive information from your guides through the Holy Spirit of God telling you where you are, and what is creating the pain you are experiencing, the upheaval that you are experiencing in whatever way it manifests.

The second part of this process is to allow yourself to feel the emotions involved and to let them express and move through the body in a very energetic way.

Give yourself permission to laugh fully, to cry fully, and even to rage fully, but your rage must be expressed in a way that does not harm yourself or anyone else.

Understand that the emotional body is going through a very deep cleansing and clearing process at this time; and the molecular structure of your body is also undergoing a dramatic shift at this time. In many ways, it is very natural to simply feel you are going through a profound change, that you are being changed at your core. This is the truth.

For life on the Earth must manifest on a new foundation. The foundation in the past has been the foundation that was created from the feelings regarding the initial separation. That foundation is guilt and self-hatred, and all around you, you see reflections of this.

As the energy of God moves into the energy field of the Earth, and into the energy field of humanity, it must create a new foundation of unconditional, loving acceptance.

If there are aspects of the self that you do not love and accept, they will be made very, very clear to you; not in a way that will manifest as painful—unless you ignore the signs or the warning signals.

This is why we say to you, that you must pay very, very close attention to what you are feeling and to what you experience every day.

Know that you have tremendous help surrounding you within your energy field. We are very ready to give you whatever we can in the way of healing energy, in the way of information to help you.

We want you to know you are to be free on the Earth, and your energy fields are to radiate with love and light. You are truly to experience on the planet—whatever your heart desires. This is the will of God, and this is the true inheritance of man/woman.

But, this is only possible when man/woman joins with God in the body. That is the experience of the mystic—joining with God in the body. This joining with God in the body happens through the chakras, happens through the human body merging with the light body through the real self, or the eternal spirit.

This then creates a new being who is very unlike the unconscious human being that you believe is in existence now, or that you see now, and that you have felt yourself to be in the past.

This new being that we speak of does not feel separated from God, or from other planes of existence, in any way. This new being lives in complete and absolute health, and has the power to immediately manifest whatever is desired through the heart.

This is possible because there is no separating wall between the self and God, or between the self and the will of God.

That separating wall is guilt and guilt must be dissolved. Guilt opposes love; it opposes life; and life is what God wills for every created being.

We ask you now to receive the healing we are permitted to share with you, and bring to you from the heart of God.

Your guides step in with you now, and surround you— and we send to you a healing light from the Mother.

Now the Light of God lives within you, and as you know, it can do for you what you cannot do for yourself through the will of your own mind. Eventually, you become one with this light, but you are now in a stage where you still know yourself and experience your self as part human and part divine. The energy of God within you has the task of purifying the human self.

By purifying the human self, we mean it has the task of changing the parts of the self that are still vibrating in lovelessness, or guilt. By this we mean the parts of yourself you still do not love and accept.

When you offer those parts of the Self to the God self within you—and from your own free will ask that they be changed that you be changed—a process of transformation does open within you.

Opening to the Christ Within

I will now focus on opening to the Christ within. You have studied the false ego self and you understand it quite deeply. You understand its darkness and you understand its insanity.

What you are here to do on the planet now though is to prepare yourself to open to the Christ self to the son or daughter of God that lives within your soul. You are to allow this self to manifest in your life on the Earth plane. That is the experience of mastery.

The full presence of God has been absent on this planet. God's Light has been here to a limited degree. But this planet has been controlled and dominated by forces of darkness.

As we send more and more of the energy of God into this planet, the forces of darkness must leave. The dark forces exist as a collective consciousness that surrounds the energy field of the Earth. But they also exist within each human being as the false ego self. So the great purification happening is that each soul is given the path of healing the false ego within.

If a soul is not ready to heal the false ego within, as we have said before, they will not be able to remain on the planet. For this planet must continue on a path of love, and so the beings that live on this planet must be committed to love.

We would like to open the energy of this class by having you each meditate on the statement:

"I commit myself to love."

B r e a t h e and feel the energy that opens within your body. This is important.

The forces of darkness have distorted all spiritual paths that have come to the Earth so far. One of the great distortions on the Earth has been the belief that the body is separate from God. So when we work with you we are always asking you to feel the vibration in your body, because we are facilitating the birth of the real self or the birth of Christ or the birth of God within your physical body.

The spiritual teachings that have been distorted by the dark forces have done great damage. One of the ways this damage has been done is through the disempowerment of humanity by teaching humanity that their sexuality is outside of God.

We ask you to listen to these words through your heart to understand that creativity is sexuality, they are the same energy. Just meditate on that for a few moments. And the essence of God is sexuality. God is creativity; creativity is sexuality. The essence of God is sexuality. If the essence of God is sexuality, then the essence of life itself is sexuality and your essence is sexuality. The essence of man is sexuality. Breathe and let the energy move through you.

Understand if you are taught, as has been the case for eons of time, your essence is outside of God, then that essence becomes covered with the consciousness of shame and guilt and darkness, then the form that manifests from your essence will be distorted.

Hence, all the sickness, suffering, aging, decay that comes from the distortion of sexuality is the shame and guilt that has been put upon the essence of man.

As your guides and teachers from the world of spirit we must correct this damage. The correction comes, through teaching you to find the places within yourself where you have learned to not love yourself and to bring love directly to those places, so you become whole. Then you become the Christ.

In order to understand what the Christ is let us look at the story of the man Jesus. The Christ is all-powerful. Within the Christ there is a direct line to the Father/Mother. The Father/Mother's voice is always heard within and becomes the guiding force within the life experience.

The energy or the power of the Father/Mother comes through the Christ channel; therefore there is the ability to heal.

There is the ability to create or perform miracles. A miracle is simply an act that steps outside the laws of time and space as you know them on the Earth plane. A miracle happens because the consciousness that creates the miracle is in the realm of God, the creator of all life. In that realm there is only one law and that law is love.

Our work is to open each human being who wants to be open to this Christ self. When you open to your Christ self you are always living in abundance because you are not cut off from the flow of the life force, from the Father/Mother. It then becomes impossible to be sick. It becomes impossible to experience lack. You then live in the way that God created us to live and that is in peace, happiness and abundance, where whatever is desired to open to greater happiness instantly manifests.

We have expressed before the fact when individual beings are vibrating in happiness and fulfillment, the Light of God itself expands. If you look at all of this and understand it you will see how God has been missing on the Earth plane and how the will of God has not manifested here. Everything here on the Earth is backward and because of the influences of the dark forces and the will of each human's false ego to have a kingdom here on the Earth. All of this must change.

You are at the end of a long journey, for your intention has always been to evolve out of the false ego self and to open to the Christ self. As we have said before, there is a possibility of that occurring for you right here and right now in this incarnation.

As you move into the holiday season on the Earth plane, the Earth will be flooded with even more light, even more love. This will bring divine manifestations to those of you who are open. Your ability to commune and communicate with us from the world of spirit will intensify. You will release patterns that you have held for long periods of time. But most importantly, you will feel an inner sense of love and peace that will grow and grow.

If you have parts of the self that are not cleared and not vibrating in love, they will come up quite strongly for you to work with. But we will be there to help you work through whatever it is you need to work through.

It all boils down to the teaching Michael has given for each of us to affirm:

"I am here on the Earth to learn the lesson of loving an accepting myself completely. I joyously open to learn that lesson. When I have learned that lesson I will have no more problems and no more need for healing."

Beloved brothers and sisters, that is the will of God; that you have no more problems and no more need for healing.

When this will is manifested, you then move to a new level of life where life becomes about exploring love and creativity, and that is the will of God.

Any spiritual teaching that tells you life must be about a long series of problems you must overcome in order to reach God is a false teaching.

There is an end to all of this. That end doesn't mean the world ends or your life on the planet ends, it means that you have reached the consciousness of unconditional love for yourself and you then do not have to struggle through inner Karma. You can then open to a life of creativity and joy.

God is joy. In your sexuality you experience joy. You experience something primal, something deeply loving and pleasurable. **This is God**. When you understand it is God it has the purpose of expanding you. That is the will of God, that life and creation expands and expands and expands into more and more light. That is the purpose of your sexuality. This has been distorted on the Earth plane and it is a major correction that must occur.

Self-Love and Spiritual Sexuality: The Key to Understanding, Inner Liberation and Caring for Your Psychic Self

There is a great opening occurring for you now and it is very wondrous for us to behold and we are experiencing joy at observing the liberation, the inner liberation that you are experiencing now.

The path of opening to self love is a very deep path and it is only difficult if you resist your emotional body and if you resist your feelings. If you give yourself over to your feelings and allow them to express through you, you can continue your journey and your evolution in a way that is very fulfilling for you and will become more and more easy for you to experience and live through.

The emotions in and of themselves cannot harm you at all but because you have become accustomed to living with the emotions locked within, there is a fear of approaching them, there is a fear of what the emotional body holds.

What it really holds when you go past its long held grief and anger is love. It holds the love that will literally change and save your life, for it is the love of the Mother. The love of the feminine aspect of God, the love of the mother of everything lives within your emotional body.

This love is the love that will give you love and acceptance of your physical self, your human self, your emotional self, your sensual self, your sexual self. You are to love these parts of the self and to open these parts of the self to the spirit. That is how you become whole, and how you become completely self-realized. That is how it becomes possible for the body to lose its tendency to age, decay and to die. That is how it becomes possible for the body to be able to speed its vibration to the speed of light and to ascend into other realms.

We are now going to work with you on opening to deeper love for your human physical self and its emotions and sexuality, starting with your spiritual psychic development.

As we have said above, the connection with your higher self and the connection with your guides is really your inheritance. As you develop it you will naturally open to using it to serve and help others. For naturally through this work, you open to the energy of God, and the energy of God has as its nature, the desire to reach out, to heal, to serve, to nourish, and nurture life.

Please pause for a moment and breathe in the energy that is here for you. Experience it now. Feel how it is a different energy, an energy that connects you to the Earth, an energy that connects you to your physical self. Just experience it for a few minutes in your body.

You are very naturally psychic. You are very naturally psychic because you have developed a spiritual consciousness in other lifetimes.

If you come into this life naturally psychically sensitive and spiritually developed, it is very difficult to manage your energy unless you go on a very rigorous and disciplined spiritual path.

When we say a rigorous and disciplined spiritual path, we do not mean an unpleasant spiritual path, but we mean a path where meditation, and working on the inner self and working to clear the false ego self becomes as natural and as essential as eating, sleeping, and bathing. If you are naturally psychically sensitive and open, if you do not incorporate this spiritual path work you will find it impossible to maintain your balance and equilibrium on the Earth plane.

The protection of psychic work comes when you surrender it completely to God, then we step in and guide you very carefully. We ask you over and over again to fill your auras with the energy of white light; this also protects you from any negative or what you would call low forces or energies.

The work on the false ego is essential also. For as you come to more of the feeling of love and acceptance of yourself and as your false ego is dissolved more, your vibratory rate increases and you become more compatible or receptive to the energy of God. This takes you to higher and higher realms and planes of consciousness while you experience physical life on the planet.

This is why you will go through stages where the spirit guides who are able to work with you and reach you, will shift and change according to your development and growth as a person. Is this clear to everyone?

Your protection is always to open to greater and greater love and acceptance of yourself and to again and again surrender your psychic work to the heart and will of God.

The message of *A Course in Miracles* is a message of your eternal innocence:

"I am eternally innocent and without guilt and without any reason to keep myself from experiencing life, from experiencing the Kingdom of Heaven."

We would like to focus now on the physical body and to have you understand that in truth it is nothing in and of itself but it is the form that the inner consciousness of your human self takes.

When your human self understands it is the son or daughter of God and takes on that identity, the human self loses its guilt. Then this body, this form that you have becomes enlightened, invulnerable and it becomes impossible for it to age or decay or to die.

Your sexuality though, takes place within your mind, within your spirit, within your soul, even though you experience it in your body. This is why when there is true sexual joining between two beings, they really lose sight of being specifically body identified and opens into the realm of the spirit which encompasses the body but which is so much more.

Through their sexual union, when it occurs in the willingness, to love and to truly join, God enters in and creates bliss, and that creates ecstasy. This is an experience that God would have all of humanity know about and understand and experience for through this experience, truly, God's light increases.

Clearing Yourself So You Can Receive

We bring you greetings from the Heart of God.

You are beginning to understand what is possible when your mind opens to the realm of God and you open to an understanding that your body itself is also of that realm.

What is possible then is the creation of a life in which heaven manifests for you while you are in the body and on the Earth plane. As we have said before, this is indeed and in truth the Will of God. But the energy of Lucifer or that force that negates the Will of God has been so predominant on the Earth over so many eons of time that the true Will of God has not been able to manifest until this juncture in time and space.

You who are receiving teachings here are among the brotherhood and sisterhood who will open and lead a pathway for others to follow. This pathway is the manifestation of the true God, the God of unconditional love.

Our work with you always is to open your consciousness to the places where you have shut yourself off from love, to expose those places to you and to transmute that energy through channeling energy from the Heart of God into your own energy field, which manifests through the body. The goal is, of course, to reach a place in consciousness where you have absolute and complete unconditional love for yourself.

As we have said before, the mind is the creator, the mind is the builder. The mind brings life into manifestation as it converges with the emotional body.

If your mind is saying that it wants abundance, prosperity, love and health and your emotional body is saying no I am too guilty and I am too terrified, there is not a clear channel for manifestation to occur.

The emotional body must receive healing from the Heart of God and healing through and from your own spirit.

This occurs in a way that you really cannot comprehend and in a way that you cannot understand or delineate and it is what we call a miracle. It really is the process of God opening within your mind and within your body and changing you.

You will find that as you open in deeper and deeper ways to the energy of God that you will be changed and transformed always for the better but often in ways that are unexpected.

We spoke before about the rhythmic flow of the life force into the Earth plane and into the creations of the Earth, which includes your physical body. As you have the will to open to the life force, that energy will have an effect within your body and of course within your consciousness, creating a state in which you are always becoming something new. You are always reaching into greater depth and greater love. There is truly no end to your transformation, and there is never a state in which you are finished.

You will always be becoming because that is the nature of creation, to always expand, to reach out to find new forms and new ways of being.

God Is Ecstasy

We bring to you greetings from the Heart of God. We want to take you to a new place, to a new depth of understanding of what love is.

We are bringing to Earth a new experience of life. We are bringing to the Earth plane the frequency of ecstasy. Ecstasy is God. We would like you now to meditate on that sentence.

As you take in some very full nourishing breaths you focus on the sentence, the statement, the truth:

"Ecstasy is God."

"Ecstasy is God."

We will try to the best of our ability to describe the state of ecstasy with your language.

Ecstasy is the state of soaring. It is the state of being exhilarated where you feel limitless, where you are in a transcendent cosmic experience of life.

This experience has not been known or experienced by human beings on the Earth and yet you who are working to open the self to receive the energy of God in its truth and in its depth are preparing yourself to live in that state. For this is the true *inheritance* of all created beings.

There is an energy within you that opens you to the experience of that state. The energy is your sexuality. Ecstasy is the experience of orgasm. That experience in which you transcend the limitations of your mind, your body, your human self and you experience sheer pleasure, sheer bliss.

As the human self is purified more and more its vibrational frequency changes so that it is able to sustain the state of bliss.

The human self as it is now is constructed of layers of consciousness which are in many ways the opposite of bliss. These layers of consciousness come from memories of suffering and pain and guilt and rage so pleasure is difficult for human beings to sustain. The consciousness that is the human consciousness is simply not compatible with the experience of sustained pleasure.

The real self within you always longs for pleasure and can create it for you. But you experience on the Earth plane a life in which you experience pleasure and then withdrawal from pleasure; pleasure and then pain. And always the real self is saying, "No, I do not want the pain, I want only the pleasure".

But the thought system on the Earth plane has become so imprinted and layered through the eons of time and experience you have lived through in this consciousness, you have lost the belief that it is possible to live in sustained pleasure or sustained joy.

Ask yourself now: Why not? Why isn't it possible to live in a state of sustained pleasure?

When you ask yourself this question you probably draw a blank within. That you simply haven't thought about it, you do not know. You recognize the belief that it is impossible to live in sustained pleasure is simply something you have accepted.

As mystics you are opening to an experience of God. The energy of God is not energy of the Earth. It is not the thought system of the Earth. It is something completely new and something completely radical and it will guide you into the experience of sustained pleasure.

As you go through the darkness of your pain, of your suffering, of your negation, what you are doing is you are releasing that consciousness to the light of your own being, the light of the spirit of God within you that is raising your vibrational frequency and readying you for living in first the state of sustained pleasure and then ecstasy.

You are each meant to come into union with partners who are the complements of the feminine and masculine energy within you. You are meant to come together with partners in sexual union to increase the presence of the light within the creation. All is energy, all is light, Light is love. Love is expanded through loving sexual union.

This information has not been given to the masses on the Earth plane in the past because of a force field of consciousness that is counter to life and counter to God.

You can call that force field evil, you can call it the devil, and you can call it the collective false ego. Whatever you choose to call it, you must understand that it is a very real force field that repels life and it lives within each human being.

As the energy of God comes to the planet and moves through the human self, that force field must be dissolved for you were all created to have life—and not life and death. You were created to have joy, not joy and suffering. You were created to live in oneness, not in duality.

The urge for sexual union is something that comes from the real self, the spirit, the soul, and the energy that is opened through sexual union is what the soul needs in order to sustain itself. That is why the sexual urge, the sexual energy, can never be destroyed, and why it is so powerful.

This force field of consciousness that negates life has caused you to believe that sexuality is not within the realm of God, that the physical body is not within the realm of

God. It has distorted your feelings, your perception about your very essence and given you a feeling of guilt about your very essence.

Your essence is actually the frequency of ecstasy. If you dig deeply into the self of the mass human consciousness you will find a current that says: "It is wrong for me to experience too much pleasure. It is wrong for me to live in a state of bliss, it is counter to God or it is counter to my spirituality." That is a very huge and very destructive misconception. God is ecstasy, God is pleasure. God is bliss.

We would like you now to meditate on those statements:

God is pleasure. God is bliss. God is ecstasy.
As the creation of God, my essence is pleasure.
My essence is bliss. My essence is the frequency of ecstasy.
I will accept this for myself now.

Open to these thoughts and this consciousness will now move into the cells of your body which of course are created from your consciousness, your mind. As your mind takes in these ideas they will have an effect on your body.

"I will accept the frequency of ecstasy.
Ecstasy is my birthright."

You begin to understand that in accepting this frequency, this vibration, you are accepting who you really are. This means that you will have, if you continue on this road, a different experience of life than other human beings. You will have an experience of life that is an experience of being completely free.

As you consider this, you understand, it means you are simply through your opening, one who shows the way for others.

If we tell you that the will of God is freedom and ecstasy for all created beings and you feel yourself opening to that frequency it must mean you are among the first to accept the will of God. It means that you are the spiritual leadership. If this causes any fear or discomfort, you take this time in this Holy Communion with your Creator, and with your brothers and sisters who are in this circle and the non-physical beings who are in this circle to release all fear of being yourself.

You say within yourself now the following:

Dear God, I release to you all fear of being free. I release to you all fear of living in ecstasy. I release to you all fear of my sexuality. I release to you all fear of love, all fear of pleasure and joy. I will accept my freedom.

As you breathe, work with that statement of intent:

"I will accept my freedom."

Opening to the Truth of God

We are the angels of God. When a human being prays we respond and are the vibrationally drawn to that human being.

The problem that we have is that humans do not understand truth. They hold within their minds many ideas and concepts that are the opposite of truth. These ideas and concepts are held in place by the false ego.

We have spoken much about the false ego and many of you who have studied with us through this channel, understand what the false ego is. It is an actual creative part of the self and consciousness that desires pain. This may be hard to accept, but it is true. You only have pain in your life because there is a part of you that wants it.

The truth will give you peace beyond measure and joy unending. The truth is that you are perfect and completely lovable and loved and accepted by God absolutely. Why is this so hard to absorb? You probably feel a resistance to it as you try to take it in. That resistance is your self hatred; it is your false ego. It wants to hold you hostage and has done so for a long, long time. It has held you hostage for all of your life on Earth. **You separated from God to experience life without love.**

That is what has gone on on the Earth. A part of you knows this and remembers this and is deeply ashamed and guilty over having done this.

When you read these words you will feel God's love and how much He wants you to come back and be happy. You have felt you deserved punishment for separating and you have given it to yourself in horrible ways; ways that are very painful to observe.

We have tried to help you but we can't help you if you refuse to open to truth and to own the false ego consciousness within you. This part of the self we are speaking of has remained unconscious in most of you. And it has created without your understanding why what happens to you happens. If you resist accepting this you remain stuck in your suffering. When you accept this, your heart opens in deep compassion and love for yourself and each other.

You do not have to continue as you have been. God loves you unconditionally and you <u>are</u> perfect. There are no debts to be paid. There are no tests to master. There is only the experience of allowing yourself to accept your perfection and the love of God.

We suggest that you let go of old religious concepts, for most of them have very little to do with the truth and they actually help you to maintain the power of your false ego. Hold onto anything that teaches you that you are perfect and lovable and let go of anything that says otherwise.

You do not need religion. **You need to open to God within.**

You can hear His voice directly. When you have opened to receive God in the past while your false ego was so strong in your mind you have heard God mixed in with the voice of Lucifer.

Just as we are angels who are sent to free you and love you, your false ego is aligned with Lucifer who sends beings to keep you imprisoned in suffering and struggle.

You may resist hearing this but it is true. If you open to it you will understand how religion and old religious teachings have become distorted and actually help to create pain and death.

God is life. Life! God is life in ease and abundance, joy and creativity. These words are words of truth and you will feel liberated as you open to receive them.

We know it is difficult to be a pioneer and to accept that the whole world as you know it is built on lies. It is difficult to accept that your most cherished religions have not freed you and opened you to God and given you an experience of him in reality.

Yes, it is difficult to let go of the past and accept truth. But there are questions you can ask yourself which will help you. Do you want suffering or joy? Do you want life or death? These lies of the past cannot give you joy and they cannot give you life.

Only God can give you joy and life and God is unconditional loving acceptance. To have life you must open to Him and to loving and accepting yourself unconditionally. The reason why it is so difficult to love and accept yourself unconditionally and to accept that you are perfect is because you can feel the false ego within yourself. You are very aware of this negative self within which judges and compares and condemns and hates. This self within that is angry and sadistic and masochistic.

You may ask, "How can I love myself when I have this horrible thing within me?" You can love yourself by understanding that the false ego is not who you really are. It's a self that became insane because of living for so long without God, without love. Through loving yourself you heal it and it transforms into an energy of love and compassion within you.

Freedom: What Everyone is Here For

Life is vibration. Your vibratory rate shifts and changes as you open to the light of God, and as you learn to love and accept yourself more and more.

The Light of God is love, and in order to be compatible with that Light, you must perceive yourself as lovable and worthy of love. And when you think about yourself, when you look at yourself, when you feel who you are—you must more and more have a feeling of love and acceptance for yourself.

You have within you a part of the self that it is very difficult to love and accept, and we call that part of the self the false ego. It is the negativity and resistance within. It holds within itself fear, guilt, vengefulness and many traumas from the past.

As you work with this self, you must understand it is <u>not</u> who you are. It is a part of the self that has suffered and has been deeply traumatized and hurt. Who you really are is love.

The false ego self of man en masse is being healed now on the Earth plane. So, the collective vibratory rate is being sped up. This makes it much easier for communication to occur from our realm.

For those of you who have worked to open as channels, we will be working with you quite consistently. First, to help you to free and heal yourself on the Earth, and then many of you will take on a task of service through which we will communicate and work with you and through your life, to reach your brothers and sisters on the Earth.

The collective work is the plan of salvation or the mass healing of suffering or separation on the Earth. For those souls who are ready for this experience we must provide the path for it to occur. We have said before through this channel, there are souls who are not ready for this experience, and they must grow and evolve, and live in other planes of consciousness.

We would like you to look at the purpose of your life on the Earth now as being to become completely free.

"The purpose of my life here on planet Earth is to become completely free."

Know that any experience of being imprisoned is happening within you. Our work is to open you to receive the Light of God on the deepest level of your being, so that absolute and total freedom is the result of your work on yourself.

You have begun to study in this class, a very powerful lecture called, "The Language of the Unconscious". Those of you who are here in this circle are ready to accept being co-creators, you are no longer looking outside of yourself believing there is a power outside of you that is controlling your life, or creating the experiences of your life. You are ready to accept it is always various aspects of the self that are creating what you experience.

Within the unconscious is the creative power of the false ego with its negativity, but also the creative power of the God-Self with its love, its ability to open to, and to share bliss and radiance.

The two selves manifest in any human life as a part of the self that wants to move forward in openness, joy, love and creativity and another part of the self that is saying "no" to those experiences and to those creations, basically because of guilt and fear. You must look at this other part of the self that says no to your happiness and fulfillment as being a wounded or abused child who needs deep and delicate love and care and compassion.

It is very frustrating to repeat the same patterns over and over again. To experience being stuck and not being able to move forward in the way you want to move forward. You must not let this cause you to reject yourself in anyway, or to have feelings of hatred towards the part of the self that doesn't allow you to be free. You must love and accept that self, and present that self to the power of God within you, and that is how it is healed and that is how you become whole.

All that you are is precious. All that you are is holy.

All that you are is absolutely lovable. These words are words of power. Let yourself have these thoughts:

> ***"All that I am is precious.***
> ***All that I am is holy.***
> ***All that I am is absolutely lovable."***

As these truths reach your core and you believe them, and you live them every moment of your life, you begin to say yes to everything you truly want and to everything that would bring you great happiness.

Remember that as you are happy and fulfilled—the Light of God, the Light of this entire creation expands.

Now, in your life you have all seen great change and turbulence on the Earth, and you will see great change and turbulence in the future. But, the change and turbulence has been and will be a movement toward wholeness, light and love. We are working with all souls in this area of the creation wherever there is openness, communication is happening at subconscious levels so that Light can fill the space of this section of the creation.

Please remember your personal responsibility or obligation is to free yourself.

Then as you open to more and more freedom, great light naturally manifests through you, for that is the nature of God and you become large enough spiritually to serve.

But you can only serve those who want to be served and who want to change, and who want to heal.

Let all feelings of guilt regarding those who do not want to be served, those who do not want to change, and those who do not want to be healed—let all of that guilt be released into the heart of God for it has no purpose to be.

Freedom is here for anyone and everyone who wants to be free and who is willing to do the work to open to it.

We release you to enjoy the rest of your class. Thank you for giving us this opportunity to serve you.

Be blessed and be in God forever.

Self-Work and the Stages of Growth

Whenever you call you are answered. We who are the angels of God have the task of fulfilling God's will on the

Earth plane. The will of God is freedom, joy and creativity for each manifested being, each manifested spirit.

As you know, collectively the will of God has not manifested on the Earth plane. But now is the time in your history, in your unfolding drama on this planet where the path of God to true liberation is here for anyone and everyone who seeks it and is ready to walk this path.

This path is a path into the self to find the spirit of God and to identify that spirit as being you; your true and real self. You must work through the layers of the camouflage self we call the false ego. This is a self that is insane and it was built on the desire, the insane desire to be separated from love.

The separation from Divine Love has created all of the struggle, suffering, and strife, pain, discontent, illness that manifests on your planet.

The answer to all of that is opening to the spirit of God within the mind, within the heart, within the body. And to do this, you must go through the emotional body. That is your power; that is your magnetic center. Your emotional body is the part of you that brings your consciousness into form. It must immediately release the past traumas and false impressions of guilt, unworthiness, and "badness".

We begin by giving you a statement of truth that brings with it an energy which, as you breathe, opens within your energy field and within your physical body to heal you. This, then, is true healing.

We ask you to focus on the thought:

"I am perfection." Focus right in the area of your third eye, the center of your forehead, **"I am perfection."**

Even say the words aloud and feel how it changes your energy. And b r e a t h e. Breathe that thought into your being. It moves through the third eye, embracing the mind.

"My body is perfection."

And breathe that into your body. Let the energy of this thought move through the muscles within your face.

"My body is perfection. I am perfection."

As you breathe the energy of this thought moves down through your neck and throat, as you breathe it down through your shoulders, down through your arms and fingers.

"I am perfection. My body is perfection."
"I am the manifestation of God; my body is the manifestation of God."

Breathe and let the energy move through your torso, reaching all of the organs within.

"My body is receiving healing and it is becoming whole and healthy."

Breathe and let the energy move down.

It moves down through your sexual organs and your have the thought:

"My sexuality is the expression of God.
My sexuality is the holy expression of God.
I release to the light of God all sexual guilt and sexual shame."

Breathe and let the energy move through you. It moves down through your legs and through your feet. As you breathe, you feel your real self, your God-Self, your light body coming forward.

You feel a field of energy around you. This field of energy around you is your *auric* being. It is your real self. It is the self of God.

In order to open to this self, you must call for it and you must release the impediment, which is the belief you are something less than love. These affirmations we give you which are affirmations of love, statements of truth, they open your human self to receive the light of God,

You must find your human self absolutely lovable and acceptable. You must see and feel and know the perfection within your human self before you can really open to union with God. Breathe and let the energy move through you.

We want to give to you a method of working on yourself. You see; you believe you are the false ego self until you make the effort from your true Self to open to union with the God Self. That effort is made through prayer. Prayer is the psychic statement:

"I want to be released from bondage and I want to join with the universal spirit of love which is God."

The moment any manifested being says:

"I want to join with the universal spirit of God."

Spirit opens up within them. But in order to help free the human being to create the liberation the human being seeks, that spirit must purify the human consciousness of illusion.

If you are afraid of facing your illusions then the spirit of God cannot help you, cannot release you from bondage. So you must be willing to face the pain within yourself, the guilt within yourself and the trauma within yourself from what you have experienced in the past. The past, not only of this incarnation but the past of your prior lives on the Earth plane.

When you call we are sent to you and we begin to work with your energy, to inspire your thoughts and consciousness. We guide you to the methods that you need in order to grow, to the people who can serve as your teachers and guides, to the spiritual teachings which may be in book form. The whole process is guided through our inspiration into your consciousness.

But the most important work that we do with you is the work that is done in your private time in meditation, in which we work to open you to your life lessons. You must begin with the understanding that everything you experience in your outer world is a direct manifestation of what you are holding within.

In your process of meditation we ask you to have it be not only a process in which you receive light and enter into a realm of peace and healing, but to also let it be a process in which you present your questions, in which you present your problems, not seeking an outer solution but first of all asking,

"What is it within me that is creating this? Where am I guilty? Where do I have emotions that are not freed and not moving and that are manifesting in my outer life in forms that are hurting me or that are creating unpleasantness within me?"

These are the mature questions to ask in meditation and we assure you, you will be answered. The answers will come through your heart. Meditation can be a very emotional process for you in which you feel the actual energy of God piercing your heart and so it is natural to cry at times when you meditate.

Meditation can also open you to anger. Anger that is old, anger that you were not aware of and so we advocate the release of anger through emotional release, through the voice and through the body in a way that does not harm the self or anyone else. Breathe and let the energy move through you.

If you allow yourself to be emotionally and psychically fluid in your meditation, you will heal, you will transform.

The voice for God that may manifest as a voice that is small, subtle and soft will grow larger within you as you continue your practice of meditation.

For what causes that voice to be drowned out is the will of the false ego which does not want you to be happy, to be free, to evolve.

You may ask: "Why would there be a part of me that doesn't want me to be liberated and happy?" The only answer we can give is, the false ego is insane and guilt has further distorted it, guilt over the separation, and guilt over the destructiveness of the past on the Earth plane which you cannot even consciously remember.

Now, we want to open this further and to extend the lessons we gave in this class last week. Your mind must always come from the place of knowing that you are limitless, that complete freedom is possible for you to experience in this life on the Earth plane. Complete healing and complete manifestation of life according to your own heart's desire.

This is a challenge because it has not manifested before on the Earth plane. There has never been an experience on the Earth plane when you are in human form, where you have lived from a completely liberated state of consciousness and experienced that liberation manifesting in physical reality. But it is absolutely possible when the emotional body is fully healed.

Now we want to speak briefly again about physical illness. Physical illness is simply psychic conflict or emotional energy that hasn't received enough light for freedom. The difficulty is the energies retained within are so old. Even when your consciousness has opened to light and to a new awareness, to a level of enlightenment, there is a backlog of energy within the body and the body has had to hold the pain not only of this life but of many incarnations of suffering.

So the body will often lag behind the consciousness or the mind. This is why you must always ask the body: what can I do to serve you and to promote your living in health and love? What do you need in order to feel better? The consciousness of your body will always give you answers.

It will tell you what foods you should have at what time. It will tell you if you need medicine and what that medicine should be. So know that yes, healing does come through medicine.

God uses anything that is available to promote healing for its beloved spirits who are seeking healing. Breathe and let the energy move through you.

As you allow emotions to release through the body and as you allow your body to receive light through the energy centers in meditation, healing will manifest. It is inevitable.

Question: "Do you ask your body in meditation what it needs?"

Answer: "Yes."

Question: "Can you ask at other times too?"

Answer: "Yes, the more sensitive you are, and become, the easier it is to tap into the body's consciousness and to hear what it needs at any given time. One of the most important things to give the body is sleep. This is where tremendous healing and processing can occur and this is where our major work with you is done.

The final topic we want to discuss is the stages of your growth. Your energy will continually change on your spiritual path. Your awareness continually expands and deepens. The guides who are assigned to work with you will change. You are simply to leave yourself open to this change. Do not have any rigidity of thought in your consciousness. The key to union with God, the key to joy, the key to having your life flow is openness, always being open.

This is why one of the most important spiritual

teachings that have come to your Earth recently, "A Course in Miracles" has a lesson in which the meditation is:

"I do not know what anything is for."

It opens you to allowing the spirit of God within to teach you. It also tells you in this lesson everything that happens to you, everything in the creation is ultimately for your happiness, for your enjoyment. Breathe and let the energy move through you.

Question: "When you speak of being open, how does one protect oneself from negative energies?"

Answer: "When we speak of openness, we mean the openness of mind, having no belief in limitation. We do not mean being psychically unprotected. Your protection is always to allow us to build light within your aura in meditation. But, your protection also is being attuned to your own emotional body, your own will, which always tell you what is safe for you and what is not. What will hurt you and what will help you. As you move into a holistic consciousness of self-love all of your energy is aligned in love. You love yourself so you are not drawn to anyone or anything that could hurt you in any way."

Question: "Isn't it true that some of these negative energies try to infiltrate your path?"

Answer: "Negative energies have no power unless there is lovelessness within you. We will explain this. Lovelessness not being a will to hurt others, but when you have conflicts about yourself and a lack of self love and self acceptance you are vulnerable to negative energies.

The exception is that when you go on a spiritual path, we are sent to protect you. We then understand that you are working through your inner lovelessness, your inner conflicts and so our light can protect you and keep from you any experiences that would not serve your highest good as you are in your own process of healing and transformation.

This is why when you are on a spiritual path, you may find your psychic development stopped or halted. This actually is our protecting you because you are not ready to go further until you have healed the conflict with your human self.

Feel your own healing guides working with your energy. Just let yourself experience the process.

Be blessed and be in God Forever

Mastery:

Achieving Union with God

We bring you greetings from the Heart of God and we wish at this time to extend our congratulations to you, for you have achieved a remarkable level of liberation in the recent months of your life.

The goal is complete and total union with the spirit of God within. Your goal is to achieve the consciousness of mastery, the consciousness that your elder brother Jesus exposes to you in the teaching "*A Course in Miracles*" and through what you know of his example as Biblical lore is passed down to you from generation to generation.

Do not ever believe union with God is impossible. Do not ever believe anything that has limited you or hurt you in your experience on the Earth is impossible for the power of God within you to dissolve. For we say to you once again that the God power which lives within you is the same power which created Heaven and Earth, which created the entire universe. Any limitation or aspect of your consciousness that enslaves you is certainly able to be healed by the power of God within you.

Please begin by taking in some very full but relaxed easy breaths and your own healing guides will join with you and will work with your energy.

There are many things occurring on your planet at this time, many things that are frightening and painful to observe. We want to speak to you of these things and how you are to manage your own life and your own experience in the present and in the future as the Earth continues her own process of clearance and release and opening to the healing love of God.

We have spoken of the initial separation. You are now experiencing the healing of that separation in your own life.

You are experiencing the love and energy and power of God manifesting through your body. You are experiencing your consciousness expanding so your intuitive, psychic abilities open and you truly begin to experience the truth that your mind is in reality the mind of God.

You are experiencing a path that continually exposes you to new possibilities and new experiences of reality. You are experiencing accelerated growth and you are also experiencing deeper levels of happiness, fulfillment and peace, a deeper level of healing and comfort through and from the power of God that lives within you. It is activated by your will and by your consciousness.

This tells you individually that healing is possible and it is inevitable for anyone and everyone who wills it and is willing to do the work of facing the self.

We have said before, this planet cannot be allowed to be destroyed by the will of humanity. So light, healing light, loving light will continue to flood this planet. We want you to think on these things. If healing, loving light is flooding this planet and human beings are in a consciousness of self-rejection and self-hatred, there is a conflict. Unless a human being is consciously working to open to healing and to release the aspects of self that are loveless and to free the emotional body, they will experience conflict in their life on the Earth plane; conflict that will appear devastating.

This is also happening collectively, but you must understand that each soul on subconscious levels is being given a choice and an opportunity to walk the path of God; the path of love.

If it is decided the path of love is not the path wanted or the path of love requires too much change or release of rigid patterns, then it is inevitable that suffering will occur for those souls who make that decision.

You will see this in your life and we want you to always understand that there is a loving process at work underneath anything that you see.

You will also see very powerful manifestations of God on Earth. You will see miracles. You each are and will continue to experience miracles in your own life.

You will see spiritual teachings and spiritual truth made completely available to the general populous so there will be very opportunity to heal and align with love.

You are only at the beginning of the glorious path that is in store for you. You are our channel on the Earth. You are the channel of God on the Earth, so you will feel your personal power increasing. This light that you feel within your physical body will increase and increase.

Through your physical body, light is entering into the energy field and into life on this planet. At times you will feel yourself taken into beautiful altered states of consciousness when you are not even necessarily seeking to go there and you will feel energy emanating from your energy field, from your hands, from your chakras. Know that healing is taking place, not necessarily for you but for those around you. For those around you who are calling out to God within the level of their own soul, ***God is answering them through you.***

You need only let the light and love come through you as it does in a spontaneous way.

As you each grow into more spiritual maturity, you may choose to take on a more formal task as spiritual teachers. We can work directly through your consciousness and through your energy field so you could serve others who are in need and seeking to walk the path of love, the path of God.

This is most important and holy work. We are grateful for your efforts in spiritual psychic development and the development of self as a channel for the Spirit of God to work through.

We say to you again that your first responsibility and obligation is to yourself, to free yourself, to completely heal yourself, to completely transform yourself. As this occurs you become love itself, not only in name, but also in your actual feeling about yourself.

We say to you over and over again this is your truth, this is your real identity; you are love itself.

As your healing and transformation increases and deepens you begin to feel that you are love itself. One of the principles of love is that it naturally extends itself, it must extend itself, it cannot hold back.

You will find your hearts expanding into greater and greater love for humanity and giving forth light and love will become natural and effortless to you.

You will also find your material abundance will inevitably expand as you continue to walk this path of God; for you become your true selves, a manifestation of the light of God. The Light of God is abundance and your material power on the Earth naturally increases. This also serves a great purpose in giving you freedom and power to serve the Light.

To serve the Light that heals anyone, and everyone who is ready to receive it. So the essence of our message for you is to not hold your growth back even though your growth is going to take you into uncharted territory.

We want to speak to you also on the subject of relationships. You are deeply intertwined with many,

many souls. All who are here on planet Earth are deeply intertwined with each other, in the relationships in your life, where there has been disharmony or conflict or unresolved issues in the past of this life or the past of previous incarnations. You will be confronted with souls you need to have a release with in your own heart and about your relationship with them.

It is never required that you spend physical time with or that you love from the ego self someone whose energy and whose consciousness is manifesting in a destructive way and who is not making attempts to evolve. You are never asked to do that.

What you are asked to do is to release and forgive everyone. You will experience within yourself deep times of review of your experiences in this incarnation, and any un-cleared feelings you have regarding other souls will come up for evaluation for you.

Your task is simply to present feelings that are not manifesting in love, perhaps feelings of hurt or anger or resentment, whatever those feelings are, you are not to deny them within yourself. You are to acknowledge them and feel them and then present them to the power of God within you, asking for a shift, asking for an ability to release and forgive.

You will find as you let your emotions release any charge that a relationship still holds for you, there will be a clearance, and you will eventually reach a state of peace and acceptance regarding all of your relationships. This also adds to your personal spiritual power, for much of your power has been tangled up in unresolved conflicts with others that fester in the psyche.

Another great truth that is manifesting on the Earth plane and will continue to open is the truth that sexuality is the essence of the energy of God. It is through your loving sexual union with each other you truly open to the holy spirit of God and increase the presence of Light on the planet.

More and more you will feel the heart yearn for spiritual partnership in loving sexual relationship. You will then be confronted with any blockages or fears you have regarding such union so that they can be released and you can join with your true soul companions.

This leads us to the subject of pleasure. Most of you are very clear you do not want to suffer any more, that you do not want painful experiences. At the same time there is within every human being a sense of guilt regarding pleasure, that somehow pleasure is wrong, or not deserved or not according to the will of God.

As you all know that belief about pleasure is guilt and guilt is meaningless, so your task is first of all to see. Very carefully observe in your own life, your own reaction to pleasure.

When good things open within you, when pleasurable things open within you, when they come to you, do you shrink from them? Or after you have experienced them do you have a feeling that it was too much or that it was wrong or that it was somehow bad? If that is your internal reaction know there is guilt that must be released.

The Light of God is in process of stretching you more and more and more so that you are able to take in pleasure so that eventually you will be able to live in that state and to sustain it eternally.

Your ability to receive us to hear us to have thoughts transmitted from our realm into your own consciousness will increase and increase and increase and we will guide you to the depths of transformation in your own life and to opening to greater and greater joy.

For this is truly the will of God for you. And it is our task as the angels of God to make this manifest in your life.

Observe what manifests in the future on your Earth with the upheaval and the crises and the breakdown of unloving structure. It will be necessary for you to cultivate a deeper relationship with us in our world and with others in the spiritual and mystic community on this planet.

You will then learn to support each other to nurture each other and to stand forth as elder brothers and sisters to those souls who are new to the path of God, the path of love, the path of liberation.

This is the message. This is the information we want to bring to you. You will need time to study it and to apply it to your own life and your own situation.

Epilogue

The title of this book, *On Earth...As It Is In Heaven*, expresses, I believe, the ultimate goal and purpose of our existence: to transform our present level of consciousness, which is based in separation, in order to bring Spirit and matter, Earth and Heaven, together.

Once you begin to work on this path and experience becoming happier and more at peace, once you experience yourself and your life beginning to change, you will not want to stop this work. It becomes a way of life.

The gift that this path gives to you is peace of mind and the joy of being fully alive in each moment. Work with the teachings again and again. "Seek and ye shall find."

It all begins with your desire, the desire to heal, the desire to know, the desire to open. If you are willing to let go of all you think you know and understand, God will transform your soul and you will find yourself experiencing heaven while you walk the Earth.

Thank you for sharing the journey.

God bless you.

Rev. Daniel Neusom